We carry on out there !

Best wishes

Kate

Kate Russell

101 Tips For Employers

The Briefcase Bible For Employment Questions

101 Tips For Employers
The Briefcase Bible For Employment Questions

© Kate Russell 2006

First edition 2002
Second edition 2004
Third edition 2006

http://www.russell-personnel.com

Published by
RPT Publications
9 High Street
Stony Stratford
Milton Keynes MK11 1AA

ISBN 978-0-9546054-2-1

Cover design by C Designs

Other books by the same author: A Manager's Practical Guide To Discipline - Nine Easy Steps to Becoming Decent, Legal And Fair

About the Author

Kate Russell BA (Hons), Barrister, MA

After studying for a business law degree, Kate qualified as a barrister. She moved to industry, gaining several years experience in operations, moved into human resources and later became a training specialist working in the manufacturing, distribution and service sectors.

She started Russell Personnel & Training in 1998 and now divides her time between advising small and medium sized businesses on HR issues and delivering a range of highly practical employment law awareness training to line managers, including a range of public workshops. Her unusual combination of legal background, direct line management experience and HR skills, enable Kate to present the stringent requirements of the law balanced against the realities of working life. She is a senior presenter for several companies and a popular public speaker. Kate completed a MA in strategic human resource management in 2004.

She is the author of several practical employment handbooks and e-books as well as a monthly e-newsletter, the latter document neatly combining the useful, topical and the frivolous.

For more information about Russell Personnel & Training, go to **www.russell-personnel.com**

Acknowledgements

However exciting it is to be turning a whiskery pile of notes into a proper book, there comes a time when you've lived and breathed it for so long that you want to throw the whole lot out of the window. That moment came for me at the proofing stage. Fortunately for the continued well-being of 101 Tips, various clients and friends volunteered to read the draft chapters for commonsense and typos. There were strict words about my rather random use of semi-colons and full stops, questions about content as well as some teasing about a tendency to repeat myself. I did begin to wonder if they were rather enjoying being strict with me for once! That said, their comments were all incredibly useful and I hope I have now got it about right. Their help got me to the end and I'm extremely grateful. Thank you to the following people for taking the time to read through and provide me with feedback:

Kim Brosnan, Carol Feltham-Rickard, John Langridge, John Smith, Graham Wellings, Paul Willson, Gill Eddy, Ginette Kennedy, Carolyn Alcock, Harry and Dorothy Gee, Claire Smith, Graham Dale, Rita McGee, Trevor Norgett, Alan Smart, Heather Soutar, Rita Terry and, last but not least, Dave Kinder.

Special thanks are due to Jeff Smith who helped me produce this latest edition of 101 Tips. He gave me constructive feedback about what did and didn't work, told me what I could do to make it better, as well as providing a good deal of practical advice in producing the book. I'm extremely grateful for his time, knowledge and patience.

Thanks to Annette Bulger who helped me with a number of layout issues and Caroline Massingham who designed the cover and put up with me changing my mind all the time.

To Jack
An inspiring dad!
With love and thanks

Statutory Limits

Today's limits have not been specified in this book because they go out of date so quickly.

Email **info@russell-personnel.com** for an up-to-date copy of statutory limits.

Keeping Up To Date

Keep up to date with our free e-newsletter by emailing **subscribe@russell-personnel.com**

Disclaimer

Whilst every effort has been made to ensure that the contents of the book are accurate and up-to-date, no responsibility will be accepted for any inaccuracies found.

This book should not be taken as a definitive guide or as a stand-alone document on all aspects of employment law. You should therefore seek legal advice where appropriate.

The material produced here is the property of Russell Personnel & Training and may not be reproduced without permission.

Note

For convenience and brevity I have referred to "he" and "him" throughout the book. It is intended to refer to both male and female employees.

Abbreviations

ACAS	Advice, Conciliation and Arbitration Service
APL	Additional Paternity Leave
CA	Court of Appeal
CAC	Central Arbitration Committee
DDA	Disability Discrimination Act 1995
DWP	Department of Work and Pensions
DTI	Department of Trade and Industry
EAT	Employment Appeal Tribunal
ECJ	European Court of Justice
EEA	European Economic Area
ERA	Employment Rights Act 1996
LEL	Lower Earnings Limit
SAP	Statutory Adoption Pay
SMP	Statutory Maternity Pay
SPP	Statutory Paternity Pay
SSP	Statutory Sick Pay
WFA	Work and Families Act 2006
WTR	Working Time Regulations 1998

Contents

Chapter 1   Recruitment

Chapter 2   An Introduction to Discrimination

Chapter 3   Contracts Of Employment

Chapter 4   Employment Rights

Chapter 5   Managing Absence

Chapter 6   Discipline And Grievance

Chapter 7   Termination of Contract

Chapter 8   More Tips – Legislation In The Pipeline

Introduction

Employment law is a fast changing area and looks set to remain so at present...... Many managers find that keeping up with the law is an extremely time consuming - and at times frustrating - activity.

Escalating levels of awards and constantly changing legislation make the area of employment law the daily equivalent of walking the tightrope for a busy company. All employers face issues relating to a host of laws and regulations. These include, but are not limited to unfair dismissal, sex, race, age, disability discrimination and so on. Lack of knowledge can land you in an employment tribunal, often on the losing side. Lack of intention is no defence.

There is a greater awareness amongst employees about their rights and they are being encouraged to pursue them. Even employees who have less than one year's service can make a lot of claims under areas such as unlawful discrimination, breach of contract, working time and the minimum wage.

If you've only got time for the right answers make sure you use 101 Tips For Employers! It will give you clear information in answer to your questions, help you understand the options and enable you to make the right decisions.

Using 101 Tips

This book is written for business owners, managers, supervisors and anyone else who manages people. I have written directly to you to help you understand your rights (despite much muttering by managers you **do** still have quite a lot of rights) and responsibilities. I have deliberately written as I speak, which is fairly informally, using "don't" and "can't" as well as "do not" and "cannot". 101 Tips is based on the questions and problems raised by my clients and it collects together all the information you are likely to need to manage your employees.

Starting – logically enough – with recruitment in Chapter 1, you can look at matters relating to discrimination in Chapter 2, contracts in Chapter 3 and so on, right the way through all the key issues until we reach the end of the contract in Chapter 7.

All the chapters are broken into shorter sections by subject content and these sub-headings are listed in the Contents, so you can go to exactly the section you need.

Throughout the book you'll find checklists and sections headed "actions for employers". Use these to help you ensure that you manage your employees effectively.

To help you keep up to date, register your ownership when you buy your copy of 101 Tips For Employers at **info@russell-personnel.com** and you will receive emailed updates of the statutory rates twice a year.

Chapter 1

Recruitment

Introduction

People are vital for the success of any organisation. It has been shown repeatedly that poor recruitment practices result in high turnover and absenteeism with a consequent increase in costs. If the right people are recruited in the first place they are likely to stay, fit into your organisation and work to optimum effect.

If the wrong people are recruited they will either leave or engage in unsatisfactory behaviours or conduct which means that you will have to manage them out of the business. This is time consuming and in itself carries risks.

There is no absolute guarantee of success in recruitment, but all the evidence suggests that a disciplined and systematic approach to recruitment will achieve better results.

Key elements of an effective recruitment process include:

- Confirming whether or not there is still a need for the role;
- Drawing up a person and job specification;
- Identifying the most appropriate search, advertising and a selection procedure;
- Planning the recruitment process, interviewers and timescales;
- Requesting information on experience, skills references and qualifications;
- Making informed decisions based upon careful evaluation of the information gathered.

Tip: You need to be **really** rigorous about your recruitment practices. There are a lot of bounty hunters who make it their business to trip up careless recruiters. By this I mean that it is easy to submit two apparently identical CVs, with a material difference, such as a disability. If you call in the person without the disability for interview, but not the person with a disability, it may appear that you are discriminating against disabled applicants.

1. Do You Really Need To Recruit?

If you select the right person in the first place you can avoid many later difficulties.

Tip: Don't recruit a problem!

When someone resigns or retires or leaves a post for another reason, it's a good opportunity to assess whether the vacancy still serves a purpose. Do you still need someone to do the job he was doing? These are the sorts of things to ask yourself:

- Was the previous person fully occupied?
- Is this a good opportunity to re-organise job roles?
- Is it the right time to promote somebody into the vacant position?
- Will anyone be needed in this post in the future?
- Does it fit in with your future plans?
- Could the job be split and done by present employees without overloading them?
- Was the job done by the previous person really necessary?

- Is it right to keep the tasks the previous employee was doing as one person's job?
- Were you getting value for money out of someone doing that job?
- Is this a role which could be operated flexibly?

If, after a good look at the job, you decide you do need to recruit, the next stage is to define what you are looking for by formulating a job description and a person specification. Most companies have job descriptions. Far fewer have person specifications, but if you take the time to do it you will find that you clarify your thinking, are able to justify your choices and ultimately end up by recruiting candidates who are of a higher calibre.

2. What Are You Looking For?

A job description and person specification will help you focus on the job and identify the ideal job-holder.

Job Description

Job descriptions give an outline of the type of tasks and responsibilities which make up the job. It doesn't have to be lengthy or complex (although this will depend on the nature of the job).

It would normally include the following:

- Job title;
- Department;
- Role the job-holder reports to;
- Summary and purpose of main job role;
- Key tasks;
- Any special circumstances, for example, having to travel away from home.

Always make sure that the job description includes a catch-all phrase stating that the job holder is required to carry out any other reasonable request by management. While there is an implied duty upon every employee to carry out reasonable management requests, it makes life much easier if you spell it out.

Tip: One way in which you can add flesh to the bones of a job description is to write "A day in the life" of the job holder so that applicants get a much fuller picture of what the job is like.

Person Specification

A person specification defines the qualifications, skills, knowledge, experience and qualities of the ideal job-holder. It describes the person needed to fulfil the duties in the job description. The drawing-up of a person specification is recommended in the discrimination codes of practice.

The sorts of things to consider are listed below. They will not all apply in every case!

- Physical attributes, for example, if there is some lifting involved, the job holder's physical condition must enable him to lift;
- Educational attainments, for example, a person who works in a shop must have a basic level of numeracy because he will have to handle stock and count money;
- Qualifications, for example, a chartered accountant will need to have passed the relevant exams;
- Special aptitudes, for example, a person who works in a nursery "pricking out" seedlings, must have good manual dexterity to transfer delicate plants without damaging them;
- Knowledge, skills and abilities, for example, a designer might need to have a flair with colour, or an engineer might need spatial ability;
- Competencies, for example, being detail conscious.

Decide what sort of person would be ideal for the job role in terms of thinking styles and personality. If, for example, the job is working on a production line, you would want someone who prefers routine and likes being governed by procedures. Someone with the opposite preference, the type of person who enjoys lots of change and variety and doing things in new ways, would be unlikely to stay long in the job.

Once you have decided what qualities the ideal candidate will bring to the job, consider what is **essential** as opposed to what is merely **desirable**. Many people make the mistake of including in the essential category matters which are merely desirable. It is only essential if without that criterion the candidate simply would not be able to do the job.

You have to be able to justify your selection criteria in objective business terms. Setting unnecessary standards for qualifications, experience or personal qualities may be indirectly discriminatory. If you can't objectively justify criteria you may face a claim for unlawful discrimination.

Tip: You can use these documents to help you write your advertisement, the shortlist and even your interview questions.

3. Advertising

If you decide that you need to fill a vacancy, you will have to carry out a broad trawl of available candidates. There is no legal requirement to advertise and sometimes there will be an internal candidate who has already been identified as a suitable person for the job. Despite this, you should be able to show that your normal practice is to give a range of suitable applicants the opportunity to register their interest with you. Most companies will do this by placing an advert either in a newspaper or on the web.

Consider whether placing an advert is the best route to attract suitable candidates. Advertising can be expensive (c£20K in a Sunday paper, £400 in a local paper). Other options are company notice boards, job centres, internet, intranet, internal advertisements and offering "bounties" to existing staff (nothing to do with coconut bars, these are merely rewards for introducing applicants) to existing staff.

The sort of information applicants want to know about includes:

- Job title;
- Some information about the job;
- Where it is based and whether there will be any travel;
- Salary range;
- Essential requirements of job-holder;
- How to apply;
- Recruitment process to be used.

Advertising is expensive so if you include a reference to a web site you can include some of the information there. You can also provide an information pack for applicants to download.

The things that you should include in an advert are:

- Job title;
- Some information about the job;
- Salary range;
- Two or three of the essential requirements;
- How to apply.

Tip: Use the **A-I-D-A** formula to draw the eye. Put in something which will **Attract** and **Interest** applicants and stimulate their **Desire** to find out more. The last A relates to **Action**. Once they are attracted and interested, applicants need to know what to do to apply.

Think carefully about how job seekers will respond to what is in your advert. You want to ensure that the type of people you are looking for will be drawn to the advert, so describe the job in terms that will be attractive to the desired personality type.

If it is a production line job, for example, use words such as "stable long-term employment offered...". Don't use terms such as "thinking on your feet" or "initiative" as this would attract people who like to do things differently, which is not necessarily desirable on a production line. Even the way people are asked to respond to the advert can be used to pre-select. If you are looking for a salesperson, ask applicants to phone your office. If doing this is outside their comfort zone, they are unlikely to be the kind of person who would succeed at sales.

Avoid words like "junior", "mature", or "senior", to indicate that you are looking for people in a particular age group. Saying something like "this is a junior position in the division," or "this is a senior position in the company" or using titles such as "Junior Sales Clerk" or "Senior Officer" is acceptable because you are simply indicating the position's level in the hierarchy.

Avoid asking for experience unless it is reasonable and justifiable. If you ask for a particular level of experience it may be discriminatory because it favours older or younger age groups. For some jobs, you will be able to clearly show that the particular job requires either a set amount or else a lack of experience. In these cases it will be acceptable to stipulate this. In most cases it might be better to ask for a particular type of experience. For example, it might be better to ask for "successful sales experience in a number of different settings" or alternatively "wide-ranging" or "considerable" sales experience' rather than "ten years' sales experience."

The same thinking applies to qualifications. You should only require qualifications if you can show that the qualifications specified are reasonable in all the circumstances for that particular job. This is so because a qualification requirement is more likely to adversely impact on younger people. In other words, if you ask for qualifications that take time to acquire, make sure that these qualifications are necessary and appropriate for the job for which you're recruiting, rather than just something you think might produce a better type of applicant.

There are also some qualifications that only younger people will have (for example, media studies). Consequently, if you make a qualification in media studies part of your selection criteria, it is likely to discriminate against older workers. In these circumstances ensure that you allow for equivalent experience as well to enable older candidates to apply for the position.

4. Decide On Your Recruitment Process

Decide how you want applicants to supply their information. There is an increasing range of choices including CV format, paper or on-line applications, with additional supporting documentation. Bear in mind that a web-only process may arguably discriminate against older workers. You may decide that you want to use tests or personality profiling as part of the selection process and you need to consider what will be appropriate.

Application Forms v CVs

The recruitment process involves a good deal of data collection. Conventionally this is submitted either via application forms or CVs.

Application forms can be designed to collect the exact data you require so the form rather than the applicant determines what information is included. It is also much easier to compare information submitted by applicants when it is all in a standard format.

In the ideal world an applicant will design and submit his CV around each individual job applied for. Needless to say this doesn't often happen. As a result many CVs give far more information than is needed, but it is not necessarily the information you need to make a decision about whether to keep the applicant in the selection process. Because the information is not presented in a standard format you do have to read it carefully to ensure that you find the relevant information and identify any areas for concern.

Health Screening

Including a health screening questionnaire as part of the initial data collection process is a good idea. Your questions should be appropriate and relevant to the job applied for and they should not be excessive in their probing. For example, it would be quite appropriate to include a question about back and joint problems if a job involved some degree of lifting which could not be mechanised.

Information collected about health, both physical or mental, is covered by the Data Protection Act and you must acquire express written permission to allow you to collect and process it.

Equal Opportunity Monitoring

Equal opportunity questionnaires are issued by many organisations as part of the data collection in their recruitment process. There's no legal requirement to do so, so why do it?

Without monitoring, you won't know whether you are truly operating in a lawful and non-discriminatory way.

Monitoring can tell you how effectively you are trawling the market for candidates and whether you are offering equality of opportunity and treatment across the board. It can also tell you how and why you are falling short of this ideal. You can then concentrate on finding solutions and making changes, rather than using guesswork or assumptions. For example, an organisation that encourages job applications from under-represented groups may be wasting its time and money (and possibly doing more harm than good) if the real reason for their under-representation is that they are already applying but being rejected for some reason.

Monitoring can spot the barriers that are preventing you from making use of available talent. It also helps you to avoid what could be costly complaints of discrimination, by making sure that you pick up and tackle problems at an early stage and this enhances your reputation as a fair employer.

Selection Methods

When you shortlist applicants for interview, use the job description and person specification as a basis for selection. There is no point in interviewing anyone who doesn't meet your minimum essential criteria. Keep a record of your shortlist decisions. You may have to justify why you didn't select an applicant at some point.

5. To Interview Or Not To Interview?

Badly done, interviews used in isolation are one of the least reliable ways of predicting future success in a job. It can be as low as 25% accuracy rate.

If you use job descriptions and a person specification, prepare your questions around competencies and behaviours, the reliability improves significantly. Skilful interviewers can be as accurate as 70%.

You can further improve your chances of recruiting the right person at interview by using additional methods of testing an applicant's suitability. Tests that relate directly to the type of work to be undertaken can increase your knowledge of the candidate's skills and abilities.

When selecting an applicant, always keep in mind that you may be asked for feedback. If you can't justify the reasons for rejecting an applicant to yourself, it will be far harder to do so to the unsuccessful applicant. Bear in mind that if you haven't probed for information on a particular subject, you can't assume one way or another that the applicant has - or does not have - a particular quality or skill.

Preparation For An Interview

Make sure that:

- Letters inviting an applicant to interview are correctly addressed and contain accurate information;

- You ask applicants to contact you to confirm their attendance at interviews;
- You ask applicants to bring in evidence of their eligibility to work in the UK and to indicate if they have any condition of which you are unaware and for which adjustments may need to be made;
- All communications are kept confidential. If you need to ring an applicant at work, give your name, but not your company name;
- Where applicable you should give front-of-house staff a list of names of those invited to attend interviews. Make sure that the list of names is kept confidential and is not shown to the applicants;
- Refreshments and company reading materials are provided for applicants whilst they are waiting;
- Discriminatory questions and references are avoided;
- Interview notes are kept;
- You create a short list of technical questions to put to all applicants and score their responses;
- You prepare questions that explore the applicants' background and experience;
- You arrange for a colleague to take notes.

Tip: This tip was from an associate who does a lot of recruitment. If you have several applications for a position and there are two applicants with the same name, do ensure that you invite the right one for interview. Apparently one of her clients had two Joe Bloggs applying for the same job and they invited the wrong Joe in for interview. It was dreadfully embarrassing!

The Dos And Don'ts Of Questioning

Do:

- Keep questions relevant, i.e. make them relevant to the job;
- Prepare in advance questions that explore the applicants' background and experience;
- Write down the answers;
- Use open and behavioural questions. Open questions encourage the applicant to talk freely. Behavioural questions ask applicants to describe specific past situations where they may have used the behaviour you are trying to assess. For example, "tell me about a time you had to deal with a customer who had received poor service";
- Listen carefully to the answers and probe for more information.

Don't:

- Ask questions about such things as childcare arrangements, marital status, religion, sexual orientation or age. If the job requires travel and overnight stays away from home, set that out as a statement and ask if the applicant can meet the requirement;
- Ask hypothetical questions. The answers won't tell about any actual behaviours only what the applicant thinks he might do in a given set of circumstances;

- Ask discriminatory questions and/or make discriminatory allusions;
- Make inappropriate small talk or jokes.

Tip: You don't have to ask all the applicants the same questions, but if you do it's easier to compare the answers.

See Chapter 6 for more details of question technique.

6. Data Protection Act 1998

Make sure that you only collect data that is relevant.

You will need to collect different data at different times. For example, ask about skills, qualifications and experience prior to interview because you need the information to assess whether an applicant can do the job.

Don't ask for information that you don't yet need. For example, in most cases there will be no need to find out about dependents at the initial stage. This may become relevant later on if you offer benefits which include benefits to dependents such as medical insurance.

Since the Act became law, stricter rules apply to the processing of sensitive personal data, much of which may be collected at the recruitment stage. This includes information relating to the data subject's racial or ethnic origin, political opinions, religious beliefs, sex life, health, trade union membership and criminal convictions. If the data is sensitive and personal, the employee responsible for data control (the data controller) must obtain the explicit consent of the data subject, or else show that processing is necessary under other criteria. To meet this requirement, you need specific written consent or an opt-in agreement and this has implications for recruitment. Think about including a clause in your application forms seeking consent to gather and process sensitive personal data for the purposes of selection and employment.

Make sure that data is kept secure and confidential at all times. For example, application forms and CVs should be kept locked away.

Note that under the Data Protection Act applicants can ask to see a copy of your notes. This means that you have to be very disciplined and objective in your note taking.

Tip: Don't make notes such as "Has a moustache - likely to be the aggressive type" or "Beard – something to hide". Where it's relevant to do so it's quite fair to make an objective assessment of a applicant's appearance and write "Wearing jeans with holes in the knees". You should not merely write "scruffy".

7. Collecting Data For Selection Purposes

Small Talk

You will probably need to make a bit of small talk between collecting your interviewee from reception or for the first minute or two of the interview. Small talk should be just that – non-threatening and uncontroversial chat.

Tip: Topics that you can always rely on to be safe – if dull – are the weather and the journey to the interview.

Interviewing

Interviews need to be structured, as this helps both you and your interviewee. The opening and closing phases will be brief, but they are important.

You should aim to talk for no more than 40 per cent of the time, throughout the interview.

It's useful to interview in pairs. One of you does most of the questioning and probing, the other concentrates on taking notes, though it is open to him to ask questions where he feels it is appropriate.

Your note taker should make notes of your questions and the answers, making sure that his notes are objective and accurate.

During the interview, avoid making promises that can't be kept as they may be legally binding.

Stage 1

Introduce yourself, and then outline the format of the interview. Tell the applicant what to expect, how long the interview will last, what you want of him and what you will tell him.

Tell him that you will be taking notes so that you can keep an accurate record of what he has said in the interview.

Build rapport. A good way to do this is to look at the candidate details you have in front of you and pick out the things that naturally interest you so that you can talk about them. Keep this very brief.

Stage 2

Gather information systematically. Question the applicant in a methodical way and thoroughly probe the competencies and personality traits you have decided to explore. Do not finish questioning until you have got the information you need.

Your note taker should record as accurately as possible the key points of what the applicant says. The pace of the interview will be guided by the note taker, so take your time and allow the note taker to keep up with what is being said. Don't try to do everything at once.

Control the interview. Remember you are in charge. If the applicant is not going into enough detail, ask him to expand on what is being said. If he is talking too much, ask him just to give you the important points.

Stage 3

Check that you have asked all the questions you wanted to ask. Look through your notes and do not finish the interview until you have asked all the questions you planned.

Tell the applicant what the next stage of the process is and when he will be hearing from you.

Allow him to ask any final questions of you.

Thank him and say goodbye.

Tip: Avoid the 30 second assessment. Too many interviewers pride themselves on their ability to judge a candidate immediately. All you really know about someone after 30 seconds is how he looks and sounds. You don't know anything about his ability to do the job.

If after collecting evidence you still have a gut feeling about the applicant, explore the feeling through questions.

Put aside your immediate impression and look for evidence to confirm or deny that the applicant has the appropriate skills. Compare his answers with the criteria needed for the job.

Testing

The more information you gather the better informed you are likely to be about your applicants. Many employers use tests to assess aptitudes. Work-based tests, for example, a typing test for secretarial or other clerical staff, can be helpful in determining actual levels of skill, speed and accuracy.

Make sure any tests used are relevant to the job and are properly validated. Use them consistently and do not apply them in a discriminatory way.

Example

Mrs Mallidi was a postal worker of Indian origin. She was asked to take a written aptitude test in order to remain in employment, when a number of comparable white employees were given temporary or permanent contracts without having to take a test. Mrs Mallidi complained of racial discrimination to her employer, but her manager failed to investigate the matter seriously. The employment tribunal found this failure to address legitimate complaints to be direct discrimination on grounds of race. She had received less favourable treatment than her white counterparts and was awarded £19,757.19 in damages. Mallidi v Post Office [2000]

Tip: If an applicant may be at a disadvantage in the performing of tests, for example, if he has a disability or English is not his first language, make adjustments to help him.

8. After The Interview

- Keep records of interviews for up to six months as they can be evidence if you go to tribunal;
- Be prepared to give objective feedback if it is asked for;
- Following the interviews, send out rejection letters to unsuccessful applicants as soon as possible. Failure to close in a prompt and courteous way is one of the main complaints from applicants;
- Arrange second interviews (if appropriate) and invite applicants to attend;
- Alternatively, contact and make a verbal offer, then send out a written job offer. Both offers should specifically state that they are conditional upon the receipt of references satisfactory to the company;
- Take up references.

9. References

There are all sorts of rumours and misinformation about references, so much so that I have included some additional detail about giving references at the end of the chapter.

If you are recruiting someone always take up references. Do not trust your instincts. One of my clients took on a woman without checking her references because he was so impressed with her. She was a very plausible applicant. In fact it emerged later she had been sacked from every job she had ever held and her CV was a tissue of lies (embellishment by job applicants is not unusual). She even tried – albeit unsuccessfully – to take the company to tribunal. Overall, it cost my client about £4,000 and a great deal of angst and management time to conclude the case.

You can ask for information which should support the applicant's statements. If there's a discrepancy, then check it out.

The type of information you can ask for is as follows:

- Start and end dates;
- Capacity in which employed;
- Number of days of sickness absence;
- Whether there were any disciplinary warnings live on the file at the time of termination;
- Whether the employee resigned or was dismissed;
- Performance appraisal rating.

Actions for employers:

- Obtain written permission to write to the referee;
- Check prior employment status;
- Ensure confidentiality;
- Ask questions;
- Verify salary information;
- Document all reference responses.

10. The Asylum and Immigration Act 1996

From 1 May 2004 you have been obliged to take more stringent steps to ensure you don't employ anyone illegally. EC members are automatically entitled to work in the UK. If you recruit someone who does not have legal permission to work in the UK you will be criminally liable for a fine of up to £5,000 for each illegal worker employed. The Act puts the onus on you to make the checks.

To avoid committing a criminal offence, you should ask all successful applicants to provide proof of eligibility from any one of the documents listed in the relevant code of practice and keep a copy on file. This may provide a defence in the case of unintentional breach.

Any one of the following documents will provide a defence if you check and copy them:

- A passport showing that the holder is a British citizen, or has the right of abode in the UK;
- A document showing the holder is a national of an EEA country or Switzerland. This must be a national passport or national identity card;
- A residence permit issued by the Home Office to a national from an EEA country or Switzerland;
- A passport or other document issued by the Home Office which has an endorsement stating that the holder has a current right of residence in the UK as the family member of a

national from an EEA country or Switzerland
who is resident in the UK;

- A passport or other travel document endorsed
to show that the holder can stay indefinitely in
the UK or has no time limit on their stay;

- A passport or other travel document endorsed
to show that the holder can stay in the UK and
that this endorsement allows the holder to do
the type of work you are offering if they do
not have a work permit;

- An Application Registration Card issued by
the Home Office to an asylum seeker stating
that the holder of the Card is permitted to take
employment.

Alternatively, you can check and copy the following
combinations of documents.

List 1

A document giving the person's permanent National
Insurance Number and name. This could be a P45, a
P60, a National Insurance card or a letter from a
Government agency. (The NI number will not be
valid if it begins with the letters TN, or ends in a
letter from E to Z inclusive). In addition you should
also check *one* of the following documents:

- A full birth certificate issued in the UK, which
includes the names of the holder's parents;

- A birth certificate issued in the Channel
Islands, the Isle of Man or Ireland;

- A certificate of registration or naturalisation
stating that the holder is a British citizen;

- A letter issued by the Home Office to the holder which indicates that the person named in it can stay indefinitely in the UK or has no time limit on their stay;
- An Immigration Status Document issued by the Home Office to the holder with an endorsement, indicating that the person named in it can stay indefinitely in the UK or has no time limit on their stay;
- A letter issued by the Home Office to the holder which indicates that the person named in it can stay in the United Kingdom, and this allows them to do the type of work you are offering;
- An Immigration Status Document issued by the Home Office to the holder with an endorsement indicating that the person named in it can stay in the UK, which allows them to do the type of work you are offering.

List 2

A work permit or other approval to take employment issued by Work Permits UK. In addition, you should also check one of the following documents:

- A passport or other travel document endorsed to show that the holder is able to stay in the UK and can take the work permit employment in question;
- A letter issued by the Home Office to the holder confirming that the person named in it is able to stay in the UK and can take the work permit employment in question.

N.B. It is not a defence if you see one document from the first combination and one from the second combination.

Tip: Ask candidates who are coming in for interview to bring evidence of their eligibility to work in the UK. These should be original documents and you must take a copy.

On 1st May 2004 a further 10 countries joined the EU. Nationals from all ten of these countries are free to come and work in the UK. The Government has set up a new Workers Registration Scheme to monitor participation in the UK labour market of the workers from the Czech Republic, Estonia, Hungary, Latvia, Lithuania, Poland, Slovakia, and Slovenia. You need to ensure that a person from one in of these eight countries registers with the Home Office, unless they are exempt from the requirement to do so. Those from Cyprus and Malta will not be required to register.

Bulgaria and Romania are negotiating to join the EU in 2007.

The Immigration, Asylum and Nationality Act 2006 will come into force in 2008 and will replace the current system with two new penalties. The first is a civil penalty of £2000 per illegal worker. The second will be for a new offence of knowingly employing an adult who is working illegally. This will render the person responsible in the employing organisation for a fine or up to two years in prison.

Actions for employers:

- Ensure that the appropriate checks have been carried out and copies taken;
- Check that there is a contractual obligation in any agreements you have with employment agencies for the agencies to carry out the checks and to keep evidence that this has been done;
- Insert a clause in the agreement allowing you to turn up and carry out spot checks;
- Include an indemnity clause that would allow your organisation to recoup any reasonable losses it may incur by having to deal with illegal workers found on its premises.

The Home Office provides an "Employers Helpline", (telephone number 0845 010 6677), for additional guidance.

11. Rehabilitation Of Offenders Act 1974

The Rehabilitation of Offenders Act allows anyone who has been convicted of a criminal offence and who is not convicted of a further offence during a specified period to become a "rehabilitated person" and his conviction will become "spent". This means that the conviction does not have to be declared for most purposes, such as applying for a job. The rehabilitation period depends on the sentence and runs from the date of conviction. A conviction resulting in a prison sentence of more than 30 months can never become spent. Sex offences are never spent.

Sentence	Period
Imprisonment 30 months + Sex offences	No rehabilitation period
Imprisonment between 6-30 months	10 years
Imprisonment up to 6 months	7 years
A fine or any other sentence subject to rehabilitation	5 years
Conditional discharge or probation	5 years
Absolute discharge	6 months

Similar rehabilitation periods apply to discipline or discharge from HM Services.

Under the Act, a spent conviction, or failure to disclose a spent conviction or any circumstances connected with it, is not a fair reason for dismissing or excluding a person from any office, profession, occupation or employment or for prejudicing a person in any way in any occupation or employment. There are some exceptions to the Act, which tend to relate to work with children, the sick, the disabled and the administration of justice. Where an exception applies, an individual must, if asked, disclose all convictions including spent ones.

The Criminal Records Bureau

The Criminal Records Bureau is an Executive Agency of the Home Office and provides wider access to criminal record information through its disclosure service. This service enables organisations in the public, private and voluntary sectors to make safer recruitment decisions by identifying candidates who may be unsuitable for certain work, especially that involving children or vulnerable adults.

Organisations wishing to use the service can ask successful job applicants to apply for one of two types of check. The type of check required will depend upon the nature of the position. These are called Enhanced and Standard Disclosures. Both require a fee but are free of charge to volunteers.

Tips Extra

Giving References

Subject to some important exceptions, you are not generally legally obliged to give a reference. However, there is a presumption by the courts that a reference will be given.

References <u>must</u> be given if:

- You have expressly agreed to give a reference (for example under the terms of a compromise agreement); or
- If you are under a particular legal duty to provide a reference, (for example, companies regulated by the Financial Services Authority where detailed rules about the provision of references and the form in which they must be given apply).

Also in certain circumstances a refusal to provide a reference may amount to unlawful victimisation, if the reason for the refusal is that the ex-employee has brought a claim (or done other acts) under the discrimination legislation.

Stick to the facts and don't be tempted into giving opinions which cannot be substantiated. If all else fails, you can confirm such matters as:

- Start and end dates;
- Capacity in which employed;
- Number of days of sickness absence;

- Whether there were any disciplinary warnings live on the file at the time of termination;
- Whether the employee resigned or was dismissed;
- Performance appraisal rating.

Tip: Don't volunteer any information.

Example

Mr Dike worked in the financial services industry, where special rules apply. He brought a claim for damages against his former employers and the individual director who had written his reference, Mr Rickman, when he lost the chance of a prospective new job because the reference was unfavourable. He also claimed he had become totally unemployable in his particular field as a result.

In a section for "any other comments", Mr Rickman wrote as follows:

"Mr Dike is a very difficult person with whom to work. We shall not be sorry to lose his services. We have received two complaints of sexual harassment from a secretary and an outside office cleaner. Mr Dike has been cautioned for both complaints which he denied. No further action resulted."

Although Mr Dike admitted that the complaints against him had been made, he contended that his alleged conduct did not amount to "harassment" as that term is defined in the discrimination legislation and that accordingly, the reference was misleading, inaccurate and negligently given.

The court found that every statement made in the reference was, in fact, true. In relation to the harassment issue, the court decided that it was not necessary for Mr Dike's actions to have amounted to sexual harassment under the terms of the Sex Discrimination Act, for use of that term in the reference to be acceptable. In any event, the court found that his actions towards the two women did constitute "harassment" as a reasonable person would have understood that term.   Dike v Rickman and Ziegler Rickman Ltd [2005]

It's always a good idea to add a disclaimer. For example, "The facts provided in this reference are accurate and true to the best of my knowledge and are based upon information available to me at the time of completion. The company accepts no responsibility for any damage or loss incurred as a result of acting upon this reference."

If you do not want a reference to be disclosed you should expressly state that the reference is confidential and not to be disclosed to anyone other than the person to whom it is addressed.

If you do provide a reference, you will be under a duty to the employee to take reasonable care in compiling it and verifying the information on which it is based. The reference must be true and accurate and must not give a misleading impression. Although it does not need to be full and comprehensive, any information that is missed must not have the effect of giving an unfair or misleading impression of the individual. For example, if the reference states that an individual was subject to disciplinary proceedings, it is sensible to say whether the allegations were denied and/or whether the employee resigned before the disciplinary hearing without a decision being made. You should also explain whether any investigations had been carried out.

If a reference is misleading and unfair to an employee, you will be in breach of the implied term of mutual trust and confidence. If the employee has not already resigned, this will give him grounds to resign and claim constructive dismissal, meaning that, for example, you probably won't be able to rely on any post-termination restrictive covenants.

Example

During the course of Ms Harris' employment with TSB her employer had received a number of complaints from customers about her. Ms Harris was not asked for her comments on most of those complaints and was unaware that they had been made. Ms Harris applied for a job at the Prudential whilst still employed by TSB.

The TSB provided a reference for Ms Harris stating that 17 complaints had been made against her, four of which had been upheld and eight being outstanding. The reference was entirely factual, but failed to comment on her character and ability. Unsurprisingly the Prudential's offer was withdrawn. TSB had informed Ms Harris of only two complaints and she had never been given the chance to respond to the others. She resigned and successfully claimed constructive dismissal.

The tribunal held that TSB was in fundamental breach of the implied term of mutual trust and confidence in providing a reference which mentioned complaints that they had not drawn to Ms Harris's attention and which were misleading and potentially destructive of her career. TSB Bank Plc v Harris [2000]

The employee may also be able to sue for defamation if the bad reference was given maliciously with the deliberate intention of harming his future employment prospects.

An employer has a duty of care as regards a reference provided as part of a compromise agreement.

Example

Mr Cox was negotiating a termination package following an unsuccessful promotion. Before matters were finalised his employers received information about his activities which resulted in a special audit investigation. No evidence was found of fraud.

The parties reached a settlement and a compromise agreement was signed, including an agreed reference. This said that any question about the reason for the resignation would be answered by saying that he resigned. A request for further information would be replied to with an agreed summary of his career. The summary was favourable although bland and made no reference to the dispute which led to his negotiated departure.

Mr Cox's new job was terminated after his new employer received a reference from Sun Alliance. This suggested that he had been suspended pending investigations into allegations of dishonesty and would have been dismissed, but instead had been allowed to resign. Mr Cox brought claims both for breach of the termination agreement and negligence.

The court agreed that Sun Alliance were negligent in providing a reference to subsequent employers that relied upon allegations of dishonest conduct which had not been properly investigated. For an employer to discharge the duty of care to provide an accurate and fair reference it will usually involve making reasonable inquiries into the factual basis of the statements in the reference. An employer should confine unfavourable statements about the employee to those matters they had reasonably investigated and had reasonable grounds for believing were true. An employer is not obliged to continue with an investigation after an employee has resigned. If an investigation is discontinued, unfavourable comments should be kept to matters that were investigated before resignation. Cox v Sun Alliance Life Limited [2001]

In most cases it will be clear that the recipient of a reference will act on its contents and base his decision on whether to engage the prospective new employee at least partly on the recommendations in the reference. If the new employer goes on to suffer loss as a result of relying on the reference, this may be recoverable from the ex-employer who gave the reference. So, for example, if the ex-employer negligently states that they have no reason to doubt the ex-employee's honesty and that employee goes on to steal from their subsequent employer, then the second employer could, conceivably, recover their losses from the first employer.

If an employee asks for a copy of a confidential reference which you have written about him relating to training, employment or providing a service, you do not have to provide it because of a specific exemption under the Data Protection Act. However, it may be reasonable to provide a copy of the reference if it is wholly or largely factual in nature, or if the employee is already aware of an appraisal of his work or ability that is given in it. If your appraisal system is operating properly, employees should already be aware of any concerns about their performance anyway.

References received from another person or organisation do not benefit from the specific exemption referred to above. If you hold the reference in a way that means it is covered by the Data Protection Act (i.e. if it is held in a relevant filing system) you have to consider a request for a copy under the normal rules of access. An employee can have access to information which is about him but may not necessarily have access to information about other people (including their opinion) provided in confidence.

When considering whether to disclose such references, you should take account of the following:

- Are there any express assurances of confidentiality given to the referee?

- Are there any relevant reasons the referee gives for withholding consent (you should contact the referee and ask whether he objects to his reference being disclosed)?
- What is the potential or actual effect of the reference on the employee?
- The fact that a reference must be truthful and accurate and that without access to it, the employee is not in a position to challenge its accuracy;
- Good practice suggests an employee should have already been advised of any weaknesses;
- Is there any risk to the referee?

The recommended good practice is to provide the information in a reference, or at least a substantial part of it, to the person it is about if they ask for it. Even if the referee refuses consent, this will not necessarily justify withholding the information, particularly where this has a significant impact on the employee, such as preventing him from taking up a provisional job offer. However, there may be circumstances where it would not be appropriate for an employer to release a reference, such as where there is a realistic threat of violence or intimidation by the individual towards the referee.

Consider whether it is possible to conceal the identity of the referee (although often an employee will have a good idea who has written the reference). It may be that you are able to provide a summary of the content of the reference rather than a copy of the reference itself.

Chapter 2

An Introduction To Discrimination

12. Discrimination

"Discrimination" has almost become a dirty word in recent years, but it's important to keep a sense of perspective. All we mean by "discrimination" is that we make choices, we are discerning. Think about it for a moment. Do you discriminate when you recruit your staff? Yes, you do! We all do and we need to do it to fulfil the requirements of the job. For example, if I want someone to do a driving job, the successful applicant will have to show that he is legally and medically qualified to drive. It is a reasonable and justifiable selection criterion. Not all discrimination is unlawful or even bad practice.

It is when we select or exclude applicants based on unlawful and unjustified criteria that we run into trouble. This chapter gives you a short introduction to discrimination.

Before we look at the various types and forms you should note the following:

- There is no upper compensation limit for discrimination. In several cases applicants have been awarded over £1,000,000;
- Protection against unlawful discrimination starts on day one of employment. In fact, if you include a discriminatory term in your advertisement you could be taken to tribunal by someone you've never even met (the law on discrimination covers job applicants). For example, if you advertise a job digging holes in the road, it is likely to be discriminatory to require the job-holder to read and write fluent

English. Why do you need to be able to read English to dig holes in the road? This would amount to indirect race discrimination;

- Employees, workers (for example casuals and temps) and self-employed contractors all have a statutory right not to suffer unlawful discrimination;

- Employees don't have to resign to complain to the tribunal of unlawful discrimination. They can remain in employment with you at the same time they lodge a complaint (making for a challenging situation);

- It is no defence to argue that you did not intend to discriminate. Intention, or lack of it, is not material;

- The Equality Act 2006 establishes the Commission for Equality and Human Rights (CEHR), effective from October 2007. It replaces the Equal Opportunities Commission, the Commission for Racial Equality and the Disability Rights Commission. The CEHR will work to promote equality and tackle discrimination in relation to gender, gender reassignment, disability, sexual orientation, religion or belief and age from October 2007. It will include Race by April 2009. The CEHR will also ensure compliance with the Human Rights Act 1998.

Compensation For Injury To Feelings

One of the reasons that compensation for unlawful discrimination can be high is the award for injury to feelings. The size of awards for injury to feelings can vary enormously depending on the facts of each case and on the degree of hurt, distress and humiliation caused to the complainant.

The courts have established the following guidelines:

- Awards for injury to feelings are designed to compensate the injured party fully, but not to punish the guilty party;
- An award should not be inflated by feelings of indignation at the guilty party's conduct;
- Awards should not be so low as to diminish respect legislation. On the other hand, awards should not be so excessive that they might be regarded as untaxed income;
- Awards should bear some broad general similarity to the range of awards in personal injury cases;
- Tribunals should bear in mind the value in everyday life of the sum they have in mind and the need for public respect for the level of the awards made.

In Vento v Chief Constable of Yorkshire [2002] the Court of Appeal laid out guidelines for assessing damages for injury to feelings. The court identified three broad bands of compensation for injury to feelings, namely between £15,000 and £25,000 for the most serious cases involving a lengthy campaign of discriminatory harassment, between £5,000 and £15,000 for serious cases not meriting an award in the highest band, and between £500 and £5,000 for less serious cases, such as an isolated or one-off act of discrimination. Within each band a tribunal should have considerable flexibility so as to be able to fix fair, reasonable and just compensation in the particular circumstances of the case. It will also consider how appropriate it is to award aggravated damages, and if so, in what amount, depending on the particular circumstances of the discrimination.

Example

Ms Hall worked for Broadacres Housing association. She wore a full length prosthetic in place of her right leg. Her disability made it difficult to manoeuvre and she made repeated requests to make changes in the layout of her desk so as to eliminate the need for her to turn right, which caused her pain and discomfort. No accommodation was made and Ms Hall made a claim under the Disability Discrimination Act.

The tribunal observed that the adjustments need to accommodate her were minor but because of the "heartless indifference" shown to her, she was made to feel like a pariah.

In the circumstances, the tribunal thought that the injury to feelings should fall into the highest of the three Vento bands and awarded £24,000. Hall v Broadacres Housing Association [2003]

13. Direct Discrimination

It wasn't all that long ago that it was quite usual to see adverts such as "Girl Friday", or "Man wanted to work in warehouse" and other similarly worded examples.

Direct discrimination arises where you treat a person less favourably because of his race, sex, disability, religious belief, age or sexual orientation. Adverts of the type described above would fall into this category.

14. Genuine Occupational Qualifications And Genuine Occupational Requirements

In very limited circumstances you can ask for a person of a particular sex, racial type, religious persuasion or age if it is a necessity for the jobholder to belong to that particular group.

These exceptions are known as genuine occupational qualifications (GOQs) or requirements (GORs). They are interpreted very narrowly by the courts so if you believe that your vacancy might fall into the GOQ category, it will probably be worth taking advice before inserting the advert.

Examples of GOQs - sex and race discrimination:

- Dramatic or modelling work. Authenticity, for example, female actress to play female role in a play;
- Restaurant. Authenticity, for example,. Chinese waiting staff in a Chinese restaurant;
- Personal services. Decency or privacy, for example, male/female toilet attendants or a male assistant to work in gentlemen's outfitters. Alternatively it may be a situation where for reasons of personal welfare and educational services, it is necessary for the person to have a detailed knowledge of a particular ethnic group, for example, Bengali social workers working with Bengali children going through the court system;
- Living in. The nature of the establishment makes it impractical for the employee to live in premises other than those provided by the

employer and there is no separate accommodation for each sex.

- Single sex establishments, for example, a single sex hospital.

In the more recent legislation the exceptions have been referred to as GORs. For example, it may be a genuine occupational requirement for a person to belong to a particular religious faith. Each case will have to be considered on its own facts. It may be justified, for instance, to ask for a teacher in a Catholic faith school to be a practising Catholic because he has to support and contribute to the religious environment. The same cannot be said of the groundsman who has little to do with the pupils and therefore cannot be said to support the religious ethos.

In some cases it will be acceptable to ask for a person of a certain age. For example, some driving licences require the holder to be a minimum age.

Tip: Note that it will not be acceptable to advertise for a young person just because the vacancy is in a trendy clothes shop aimed at teenagers.

15. Indirect Discrimination

Indirect discrimination arises much more often than direct discrimination and occurs in employment where a company applies a provision, criterion or practice (known as a "PCP") which applies to everyone equally, but would put certain persons of a group at a particular disadvantage, does in fact put a specific person from that group at a disadvantage and the PCP cannot be shown to be justified by the company.

An example of this would be an advertisement that says "Person wanted to work in warehouse, must be 5'10" or more", because this excludes most of the female population.

Example

Ms Edwards had worked for London Underground since 1983. She qualified as a train driver in 1987, and her baby was born in the same year. When she returned to work she was able to organise for herself a shift pattern in which she could accommodate her domestic and childcare arrangements by swapping shifts with colleagues. In 1991, London Underground wanted to reduce its costs and had a re-organisation which involved a new shift work system. This system required operators to work flexible shifts upon short notice, but the premiums for working unsocial hours were removed.

Ms Edwards had to work during the day because she had sole care of her child and under the new system it would have been considerably more difficult for her to arrange any exchange of shifts. This would mean that she would have to work longer hours than she had previously done. She was presented with the alternative of either signing an acceptance of the new roster or facing dismissal.

She complained of discrimination in the application of a condition or requirement that made it impossible for her to continue in her employment. London Underground employed over 2000 drivers, of which 21 were female. Ms Edwards was the only person who could not work the new system.

The Court of Appeal held that this was indirect sex discrimination. Ms Edwards was one of only 21 female drivers and she made up 5% of the female workforce. If one man had not been able to comply, the proportion of men unable to comply would have been well under 1%. Additionally, the employer had failed to investigate her position or to discuss any alternatives and this was not the act of a reasonable employer. London Underground Ltd v Edwards [1998]

This case was decided under the old definition of indirect discrimination which referred to proportions affected. However, if the case were to be decided today the outcome would still have been the same.

16. Victimisation

You may well hear employees complaining that they have been victimised, by which they mean they feel they have been picked on in some way. Within the discrimination framework, "victimisation" has a very specific meaning.

It arises where a person has made an earlier complaint of unlawful discrimination and suffers less favourable treatment as a result. The complaint doesn't have to be well founded, but it does have to be made in good faith.

Example

An Asian employee complained of racial harassment by his supervisor. The company investigated and decided that there was evidence of racial harassment. They moved the Asian employee to another department. Some time later, it was discovered that by moving he had lost the opportunity to work overtime, thus suffering victimisation.

Traditionally the courts have taken the view that if a person is to take advantage of the anti-discrimination legislation, he can only make his complaint about discriminatory acts arising during employment. There was no protection if discriminatory acts took place after the end of that employment.

This was first extended in the case of victimisation following sex discrimination some years ago.

Example

Ms Coote complained that Granada had dismissed her because she was pregnant. The company settled her claim out of court. Some time after that Ms Coote found that she couldn't get another job because Granada refused to provide prospective employers with a reference. She complained that she had suffered a detriment because she couldn't get a job. She successfully argued that this was happening as a result of her earlier claim, even though Granada's refusal to provide a reference took place after her employment had ceased. Coote v Granada Hospitality Ltd [1999]

Employees have the right to complain of unlawful discrimination. If they do so and are treated less favourably in some way for raising the complaint, the court in turn will call the employer to account. Compensation for victimisation carries punitive damages, that is, damages intended to punish the employer. In this case Ms Coote was awarded over £200,000.

A series of House of Lords decisions has confirmed that it is possible for former employees to bring successful claims of unlawful discrimination where the acts of discrimination had taken place after employment has ended.

Subsequent legislation has enshrined the employer's duty not to discriminate against a person, even where the employment relationship has terminated.

17. Harassment And Bullying

Harassment and bullying are worryingly common in the UK. They are destructive, unpleasant and unlawful. Make sure that you have a discrimination, bullying and harassment policy, which says that you will not tolerate unacceptable behaviour and that you will investigate and deal promptly, thoroughly and fairly with incidences of bullying and harassment according to recognised and agreed procedures.

Your policy should include some examples of discrimination, bullying and harassment and state that such behaviour is not acceptable. It should provide a recognised and agreed course of action to be taken should any employee behave in an unacceptable manner.

Matters covered should include language, which includes workplace banter, and conduct.

A policy alone will not protect you. It's up to you to ensure it is properly implemented, monitored, followed through and disciplinary action taken where necessary.

Don't wait for a complaint to be made. If you become aware of any potential issues, investigate and take appropriate action to manage it.

Example

One manager told the following story. At his site for several years there was a black employee, known to all as "Sooty". The manager was very uncomfortable with this and he had asked the employee how he felt about being called by this nickname. The employee replied that he was quite happy about it, saying that even his family called him by this name. The manager was still, rightly, very uncomfortable with the situation. However, this had been going on for years. Rather than rock the boat, the company took a pragmatic approach and wrote to him confirming the conversation and pointing out that if at any time he changed his mind, he must advise them and they would address the matter immediately. This will not protect them if "Sooty" does change his mind and claims racial harassment, but it may reduce their risk and liability somewhat.

Tip: Don't allow unsuitable nicknames to be used in the workplace. It's much harder to discourage the practice in a company where the use of nicknames has become commonplace, than to stop isolated incidents.

Harassment

There is now a statutory definition of harassment. Harassment is unwanted language or behaviour which has the purpose or effect, either of violating an individual's dignity, or creating an environment which is offensive, humiliating, degrading or intimidating.

The definition must be considered against the objective test of reasonableness. This means that while the perception of the alleged victim has to be considered, there is an objective element which considers whether others would reasonably conclude in the same circumstances that harassment has occurred.

Tip: Ensure that all complaints of harassment are properly investigated. You must be consistent in the application of your procedure.

Example

Mr Owers was a male firefighter who argued that he was treated less favourably than a female colleague who had previously made complaints about him. After the female employee had made her complaint, the two were separated and restrictions were put in place to avoid contact. Mr Owers complained that his colleague breached those in an attempt to provoke a further incident and manufacture a further complaint. The fire service took no steps to investigate his complaint. He brought a grievance which was not investigated. Mr Owers agreed to mediation as a means of resolving his colleague's complaint but this was not followed up by the employer.

The tribunal concluded that the treatment afforded to Mr Owers was less favourable compared with the comparator female colleague. Any complaint by her was investigated, whereas Mr Owers' complaint was not. An inference could be drawn that the less favourable treatment was attributable to gender. The employer had not demonstrated to the court that it had not discriminated against Mr Owers.
Owers v. Devon Fire and Rescue Service [2006]

Actions for employers:

- If an allegation is made, deal with it in accordance with your harassment policy and comply with the minimum statutory grievance and/ or discipline procedures;
- Ensure procedures apply to all staff and are followed consistently whatever the gender of the alleged victim or harasser;
- Take allegations seriously and investigate all complaints thoroughly, including complaints made by the alleged harasser;
- Ask the victim what outcome he wants (often an apology is all that's needed);
- Consider disciplinary action if appropriate;
- Support both parties and avoid pre-judging a situation by assuming a man would have carried out the alleged harassment but a woman would not;
- Exercise caution before transferring the victim of the alleged harassment. This can be done but only after consultation and with his agreement (it may otherwise be deemed to be victimisation).

Vicarious Liability

You can be liable for the wrongful acts of your employees even if you don't encourage or condone it. This is called "vicarious liability". This liability may arise where your employee engages in unlawful discrimination in the course of employment.

Example

Mr Johnson was a black prison officer. He started to have problems at work after he objected to the manhandling of a black prisoner by other prison officers.

Thereafter he was subjected to a "campaign of appalling treatment" (the tribunal's description), including racist remarks and false accusations against him. His proper duties were not allocated to him. He was warned about sickness absence, whilst a white officer with a poorer record was not warned, and he was also reported for leaving his shift early, although it was customary.

Mr Johnson complained of race discrimination against two of the prison officers who had spear-headed the campaign of harassment and the Prison Service. The tribunal awarded him £28,500 compensation, including £21,000 for injury to feelings, to reflect the fact that the campaign had lasted 18 months.

Aggravated damages of £7,500 were awarded against the employers on the grounds that whenever Mr Johnson tried to complain, his complaints were dismissed and put down to defects in his personality.

£500 for injury to feelings was awarded against the two prison officers personally. Armitage, Marsden, HM Prison Service v Johnson [1997]

You can be also vicariously liable for workplace bullying by the employees under the Protection from

Harassment Act 1997, a statute that was originally enacted to combat stalking. There does not need to be proof of personal injury and damages can be awarded for distress or anxiety.

Example

Mr Majrowski was a gay man. He made a formal complaint of harassment against his manager, whom he claimed had bullied and intimidated him. He said that the treatment was fuelled by homophobia. The Trust investigated the complaint and found that harassment had occurred. Mr Majrowski was later dismissed for an unrelated reason and four years later brought proceedings against the Trust in the county court, claiming damages for the distress, anxiety and consequential loss caused by the harassment he suffered during the course of his employment. The employer claimed that Parliament had intended to address the public order offence of stalking and the Act was not intended to apply to the workplace.

The House of Lords disagreed and unanimously held that, unless a statute expressly or impliedly indicates otherwise, the principle of vicarious liability will apply. Majrowski v Guy's and St Thomas' NHS Foundation Trust [2006]

Reasonable Practicable Steps Defence

To establish a defence against harassment you must show that you have taken such steps as are reasonably practicable to prevent the harassment. You need not actually prevent an employee making inappropriate comments to a person of a different race or gender etc. (which would be very difficult) but you must take such steps as are reasonably practicable to discourage such behaviour.

Note that having a policy by itself is not enough. If there is good reason to think that, for example, one of your managers has been harassing a junior employee, you cannot simply rely upon having a policy. More would be needed - for example, providing training for all employees so that they understand what constitutes harassment and what is expected of them. Carry out a prompt and thorough investigation and take appropriate action.

The training and monitoring element is important. It is evidence that you have properly implemented the policy.

Example

Ms Caspersz was a staff officer to the assistant chief constable, personnel and training, in the Ministry of Defence (MoD) police force. She complained that she had been subject to sexual harassment by the assistant chief constable, Mr McDermott.

Ms Caspersz claimed that Mr McDermott had made a comment to her about her "working her way through" male students at the MoD and in a separate incident, that he suggested to her that she had been able to use some MoD "indulgence" flights as she must have "stepped her way through enough pilots" to enable her to do so.

Her claims for sex and race discrimination were dismissed. The tribunal found that the MoD had done everything reasonably practicable to prevent the harassment taking place and therefore had a defence to the claim. The MoD had a Dignity at Work policy in place, which it took seriously, and had taken all reasonable steps to investigate the complaint as soon as it was made aware of the allegations relating to sexual harassment against Mr McDermott.

Her appeal was dismissed. On the facts, the MoD had satisfied the requirements of the statutory defence. Caspersz v Ministry of Defence [2006]

Bullying

Bullying differs from harassment and discrimination in that the focus is sometimes based on gender, race, or disability etc., but often it is not. The focus is often on competence, or rather the alleged lack of competence of the bullied person. There is no specific legal offence of bullying, but if you don't take steps to check bullying behaviour it may lead to the risk of constructive dismissal, breach of the health and safety at work legislation or personal injury claims.

Examples of bullying behaviour:

- Spreading malicious rumours, or insulting someone;
- Copying memos that are critical about someone to others who do not need to know;
- Ridiculing or demeaning someone, picking on them or setting them up to fail;
- Exclusion;

- Unfair treatment;
- Overbearing supervision or other misuse of power or position;
- Making threats or comments about job security without foundation;
- Deliberately undermining an employee by overloading and constant criticism;
- Preventing individuals progressing by intentionally blocking promotion or training opportunities;
- Foul and abusive language. This is not automatically unacceptable, but its use can undermine the relationship of trust and confidence between employer and employee.

Example

Mr Horkulak, a senior employee of Cantor Fitzgerald worked in a very fast moving and stressful banking environment. He was subjected to abusive language from the chief executive (known at all as the "Brooklyn Bruiser") over a long period of time. Although the use of such language was common in the workplace, the court found the relationship of trust and confidence between Mr Horkulak and his employer had broken down because of the employer's behaviour. Cantor Fitzgerald argued there was a culture of robust communications and bad language which, they said, allowed workers to let off steam. The Court of Appeal rejected that argument and stated that "the frequent use of foul and abusive language did not sanitise its effect".

Mt Horkulak was successful in showing that he was constructively dismissed and was awarded damages of almost £1m plus costs and interest. Horkulak v Cantor Fitzgerald [2005]

Actions for employers:

- Give managers training to help them spot workplace harassment and bullying and intervene to modify inappropriate behaviour;
- Provide clear guidance to your employees about what behaviour is expected and what is unacceptable;
- Monitor rates of employee turnover (it might indicate that bullying is taking place);
- Take any complaint of bullying seriously and deal with it promptly;
- In dealing with performance or conduct issues, use your disciplinary and poor-performance procedures without recourse to abusive or insulting language;
- Managers must use appropriate management styles when handling performance and conduct issues. They must understand that their position of seniority does not give them a right to abuse others;
- Make sure that your bullying and harassment policies state that abusive language to others will not be tolerated;
- Ensure that waiver claims in compromise agreements are worded so as to preclude any claim under the Protection from Harassment Act.

18. What Does Discrimination Cover?

Protection against discrimination extends across the whole of employment:

- Advertising;
- Recruitment;
- Promotion;
- Training;
- Appraisals;
- Discipline;
- Supervision;
- Selection for redundancy;
- Post-employment matters.

Burden Of Proof

Once a complainant establishes that an unlawful act of discrimination or harassment has occurred, the burden of proof shifts to the alleged discriminator. He must then prove that it is more likely than not that he did not commit the act of unlawful discrimination or harassment. If he is unable to do this, the tribunal will decide in the complainant's favour.

19. Some Forms Of Discrimination

Sex Discrimination

The Sex Discrimination Act 1975 offers protection in a variety of areas, including employment. Women and men of any age, including children are protected.

It is generally unlawful to discriminate on grounds of sex against men and women, married people or against anyone intending to undergo, undergoing or who has undergone gender reassignment (transsexuals). Since the Civil Partnership Act 2004 came into force in 2005, the same protection is given to those in a civil partnership as those who are married. Note that it is not unlawful to discriminate against a single person.

Discrimination on the grounds of pregnancy or maternity leave in employment is also unlawful. If a woman can show that 'but for' her pregnancy or maternity leave, she would not have suffered less favourable treatment, this is likely to be sex discrimination. She does not have to compare herself to how a man was or would be treated.

Recent amendments mean that discrimination after employment is now unlawful if the discrimination arises out of the employment and is closely connected to it. For example, if you fail to give a reference or give a bad reference because of someone's gender this will now be direct sex discrimination.

Changes to the Sex Discrimination Act expressly outlaw harassment.

There are four forms of harassment, as follows:

1. Sex based harassment - i.e. harassment based purely on the victim's gender. An example might be workers who deliberately keep tools on a high shelf which is not easily accessible to a female worker.

2. Harassment of a sexual nature - i.e. physical activity of a sexual nature or non-physical activity of a sexual nature such as offensive jokes or vulgar comments, for example, displaying page three pin ups.

3. Harassment on grounds of gender reassignment status.

4. Harassment on grounds of rejection of harassment, or submission to harassment.

Race Discrimination

The Race Relations Act 1976 makes discrimination by employers related to race unlawful. Protection extends to discrimination on the four grounds of race, colour, nationality, (for example, English, Scottish nationality, including citizenship) or national or ethic origins.

"Ethnic origin" is wider than race and may include religious or cultural differences. It means a segment of the population is distinguished from others by a combination of shared customs, beliefs, traditions and characteristics derived from a common or presumed common past. The question of who is protected is decided by the courts. Three groups are protected. These are Sikhs, Jews and Romany gypsies.

Changes to the definition of race discrimination means that indirect discrimination on grounds of race or ethnic or national origin now occurs when one person applies to another:

- A provision, criterion or practice which he applies to everyone; and
- The provision, criterion or practice puts (or would put) people from the person's race or ethnic or national origin at a particular disadvantage; and
- The provision, criterion or practice puts the person at a disadvantage; and
- The company cannot show that the provision, criterion or practice is a proportionate means of achieving a legitimate aim (i.e. it can't be justified).

Note, the original definition of indirect discrimination in the Race Relations Act 1976 will continue to apply in complaints of discrimination based on grounds of colour or nationality. This definition refers to a condition which applies to everyone but means that a higher proportion of a particular group are disadvantaged because they cannot comply and you cannot justify the condition.

Recent Legislation

The Employment Equality (Religion or Belief) Regulations 2003 and Employment Equality (Sexual Orientation) Regulations 2003 both became law in

December 2003. It is now unlawful for you to discriminate on grounds of religion or religious belief, philosophical belief or sexual orientation.

Both sets of regulations are similar in structure and form to the Sex Discrimination Act 1975 and the Race Relations Act 1976. Protection applies at all stages of the employment relationship – from the advertising, recruitment and selection stage, terms and conditions of employment, selection for promotion and training, through to termination of contract. Direct and indirect discrimination, victimisation and harassment on grounds of sexual orientation are all unlawful.

Discrimination On Grounds Of Religion

The Employment Equality (Religion or Belief) Regulations 2003 make it unlawful to treat an individual less favourably on the grounds of his religion or belief. This includes:

- Putting him at a disadvantage;
- Harassing him;
- Victimising him; or
- In certain circumstances, discriminating against him after the working relationship has ended.

Religion or belief is defined as being "any religion, religious belief, or similar philosophical belief". It does not, however, include philosophical or political beliefs unless they are similar to a religious belief. An example of this would be that single-issue campaigners, such as anti-abortion campaigners, will not be covered. As there is no other definition of religion or belief, the courts will have to decide matters on a case-by-case basis.

The Regulations extend to include beliefs such as Paganism and Rastafarianism, as well as the more well-known religions and faiths. It appears that workers do not have to provide evidence of their belief and it is unclear at present to what extent the religion must be followed.

The act of discrimination does not have to be based on the victim's own religion.

There haven't been many cases dealing with discrimination in grounds of religion (and none on religious or philosophical belief) to date. The best known is Khan v NIC Hygiene.

Mr Khan was dismissed after taking six weeks off for the Hajj pilgrimage to Mecca, which all Muslims are required to undertake once in their lifetime if possible. He claimed that he had booked the time off work using his 25-day holiday entitlement, plus another week's unpaid leave. He did not receive formal confirmation from the company, but had been told by his immediate line manager that if he did not hear to the contrary, he should assume his request for four weeks' annual leave, plus an additional week of unpaid leave, had been granted. He was dismissed for unauthorised absence on his return.

The tribunal found that Mr Khan was entitled to conclude that the holiday had been authorised and held that he had been unfairly dismissed and unlawfully discriminated against on the grounds of his religion. He was awarded £10,000 in compensation. Khan v NIC Hygiene [2005]

This isn't an especially important case in legal terms. Even if the issue of religious discrimination had not been raised, NIC Hygiene acted unreasonably. The response to Mr Khan's alleged breach of procedure was clearly outside the reasonable range of responses.

It's worth bearing the following in mind. There is no right to take time off to observe religious occasions. However, if your holiday policy, which on the face of it applies to everybody equally, prevents a Muslim employee from going on the Hajj pilgrimage because he has insufficient holiday entitlement, then the policy is potentially indirectly discriminatory as it puts the Muslim employee at a disadvantage because of his religion. The Regulations do not require you to grant additional time off for religious observance, but if you are faced with such a request you should consider allowing the leave to be taken and try to accommodate the request (granting a period of additional unpaid leave, if necessary) where it is reasonable and possible to do so. However, this does not mean you always have to grant leave in such circumstances.

Changes To The Definition Of Religion Or Religious Belief

The Equality Act 2006 will make some changes to the definition of religion, religious and philosophical belief. At the time of writing no date has been set for these to come into force.

The first amendment widens the meaning to cover not only those who hold a particular religion or belief, but also those who do not. So for example, if you are a devout Catholic you could argue that you are entitled to refuse a job to an applicant who does not practice religion or who holds no philosophical belief that shapes his life. Such a situation would not be covered at present. The amendment removes this loophole (although faith establishments can still use the genuine occupational requirement exemption).

The second amendment leaves out the requirement that a philosophical belief must be similar to a religious belief to come within the scope of the Regulations. Originally the DTI's guidance notes suggested that a philosophical belief had to be profound, affecting a person's life or perception of the world in order to be similar to a religious belief. Examples quoted included atheism, agnosticism, humanism, pacifism and veganism. Support for a political party or football team would not generally be covered.

The new definition of philosophical belief is broader, but only time will tell if the courts will accept that being a fanatical football supporter or an animal rights activist falls within the scope of the amended wording.

Discrimination On Grounds Of Sexuality

The Employment Equality (Sexual Orientation) Regulations 2003 make it unlawful to treat an individual less favourably on the grounds of sexual orientation. This includes:

74

- Putting him at a disadvantage;
- Harassing him;
- Victimising him; or
- In certain circumstances, discriminating against him after the working relationship has ended.

Sexual orientation is defined as orientation towards persons of the same sex (lesbians and gay men), orientation towards persons of the opposite sex (heterosexuals), or orientation towards persons of the same sex and the opposite sex (bisexuals).

The act of discrimination does not have to be based on the victim's own sexual orientation. For example, if a worker has a brother who is bisexual and the worker's colleagues tell jokes about bisexuals, the worker could bring a claim for harassment on the grounds of sexual orientation, even though the harassment was not based on his own sexual orientation. The discriminatory act also does not have to be based on an accurate perception of an individual's sexual orientation. For example, if an employee is harassed because people think he is gay, but he is not, he can still bring a claim.

The first successful claim for sexual orientation was Whitfield v Cleanaway UK [2004].

Mr Whitfield left his employment as he could no longer stand the taunts he suffered from his colleagues and complained of discrimination on grounds of sexual orientation. He said he was nicknamed "Sebastian" either because of a camp character on the comedy television programme Little

Britain or because of the character in the novel Brideshead Revisited, who was confused about his sexuality.

The company's defence was that Mr Whitfield was nicknamed Sebastian because his colleagues felt that he was posh.

The tribunal agreed with Mr Whitfield and awarded him £35,345 as compensation for constructive dismissal, harassment and discrimination. In making this award, the tribunal took into account the number and repetition of incidents. It also criticised the company for failing to accept or deal with the problem, despite previous complaints by another gay member of staff.

Please note that unlawful harassment can arise even where the remark was not directed to the alleged victim.

Example

*An arcade manager was called derogatory names relating to his sexuality by his manager Mr Quelch. In April 2004 Mr Whitehead took several weeks of sick leave following the death of his father. After Mr Whitehead's return to work he was told by a colleague that she had heard Mr Quelch referring to him as a "f****** chutney ferret". Mr Whitehead resigned a few days later.*

The tribunal found that the use of the phrase "chutney ferret" was conduct unwanted by Mr Whitehead and had the effect of violating his dignity and therefore amounted to harassment under the Sexual Orientation Regulations. He was awarded £4,000 for injury to feelings. Whitehead v Brighton Marine Palace and Pier [2004]

The Employment Equality (Age) Regulations 2006

Age discrimination became unlawful on 1 October 2006 and offers protection to people of all ages, both old and young. Employers, providers of vocational training, trade unions, professional associations, employer organisations and trustees, and managers of occupational pension schemes have to comply with the Regulations.

Age discrimination occurs when someone treats a person less favourably because of that person's age. It follows the same pattern as existing forms of discrimination law in the UK, i.e. direct and indirect discrimination, victimisation and harassment.

The Regulations cover employment and vocational training and provides the usual range of protection (Tip 18). It is unlawful to discriminate on grounds of age in the areas of recruitment, promotion, development, termination, service benefits and pay.

The Regulations introduce a default retirement age of 65 for employees (note that they do not give a default retirement age for workers such as agency staff). This will be reviewed in 2011.

As well as applying to retirement, the Regulations:

- Remove the upper age limit for unfair dismissal and redundancy rights, giving older workers the same rights to claim unfair dismissal or receive a redundancy payment as younger workers, unless there is a genuine retirement;

- Allow pay and non-pay benefits to continue which depend on length of service requirements of five years or less or which recognise and reward loyalty and experience and motivate staff;

- Remove the age limits for statutory sick pay, statutory maternity pay, statutory adoption pay and statutory paternity pay, so that the legislation for all four statutory payments applies in exactly the same way to all;

- Remove the lower and upper age limits in the statutory redundancy scheme, but leave the 20 year maximum and current age-banded system in place;

- Provide exemptions for many age-based rules in occupational pension schemes;

- Require you to write to an employee in his 65th year between 6-12 months before the retirement date to notify him of the retirement date and his right to request to work flexibly beyond this date if he wishes;

- Give employees approaching retirement the right to request to work on beyond retirement. If an employee does so you must meet to consider the request, giving him the right to be accompanied. If you refuse the request the employee has a right of appeal. The DTI guidance suggests that there is no need to give reasons for your refusal because the reason for the dismissal will be deemed to be retirement. It remains to be seen if the courts will agree.

Irish Lessons

The Irish legislation does not exactly mirror the Employment Equality (Age) Regulations but it is sufficiently similar to make it useful to look at some Irish cases.

Brendan Noonan v Accountancy Connections

The requirement was for a maximum of three years experience post-qualification. Mr Noonan had more than the three years experience required and was therefore not considered for the job. This constituted indirect discrimination. Generalisations equating length of experience with levels of skill could not be used to justify indirect discrimination.

McGarr v The Department of Finance

Mr McGarr was indirectly discriminated against when he was unable to compete for promotion because of a requirement stipulating five years' service. He was too young to have acquired the service.

A Complainant v A Company

An older man, X, worked for a younger female manager, Y. X was hostile and aggressive towards Y and repeatedly said that she was "only a young, fooling girl, more inexperienced than he". Y complained of harassment on grounds of sex and age. The court found that her complaint of discrimination was successfully made out on grounds of both sex and age.

McLoughlin v Bus Eireann

The employer's policy of not rehiring staff who had previously taken voluntary redundancy was found to be indirectly discriminatory, as it was accepted that 96% of those who had done so were over 50. The employer's proposed justification on the ground of cost was rejected.

Actions for employers:

Recruitment and selection

- Consider the implications of where you are advertising. For example, if you only advertise on the internet it might be argued that this indirectly discriminates against older people;
- Age, age-related criteria or age ranges should not be used in advertisements other than to encourage applications from age groups which do not usually apply. Where this is the case, it should be clearly stated;
- If you use a monitoring process in recruitment (not legally required but good practice and potentially very useful) state that age criteria will not be taken into account in employment decisions but used only for monitoring purposes. This information can be asked for in a 'tear-off' section of the application form and should be kept separate from the application process;

- Interviewers and those concerned with selection must not select subjectively on the basis of physical characteristics or unfounded assumptions, and must ensure their decisions are based on objective criteria, relevant to the job and merit;
- It is still acceptable to ask for dates of employment, though you should steer away from requesting the range of dates during which candidates attended school. You are not under any obligation to recruit someone who is within six months of the retirement age. The default age is 65;
- You can still ask for graduates, but make sure that you also give people without a degree but with relevant experience the opportunity to apply. Place your adverts in a way that demonstrates that you have trawled the market thoroughly;
- Avoid asking for a certain level of experience and focus on skills and competence instead;
- Some job adverts are more conceptual than facts-based and talk about wanting "dynamic", "energetic" "mature" etc. people to join the team. Alternatively they may talk about a "young company". These words (rightly or wrongly) tend to be associated with certain age groups and may be discriminatory. Avoid such words and talk more specifically about the skills sets required;
- Rejecting a candidate as "over-qualified" without a valid justification could amount to indirect discrimination against an older worker. While you may have legitimate concerns that an older worker with extensive

experience may lack motivation for the job, you will have to determine this on a case-by-case basis at interview;

- Making a stipulation that candidates have to work late or must be willing to socialise may be indirectly discriminatory (on grounds of age and sex) because this is more likely to impact adversely on those with child care commitments;

- Don't ask questions which reflect a bias against age at the interview, for example, "How would you feel about working with such a young group of people?"

Medical advice

- If you make passing a medical part of the terms of the job offer then ensure that this condition is applied to everyone, not just one group of people, likely to be older workers;

- An individual's age should not be used to make judgements about his abilities or fitness. Where such a judgement is required, an occupational health or medical practitioner should be consulted.

Environment

- Avoid allusions, jokes and other inappropriate references to age. For example, if birthday cards are given in the workplace they should be suitably decorous in tone and not make jokes about the number of candles on a birthday cake being a towering inferno;

- If colleagues socialise together try to ensure that people belonging to a certain age group aren't left out because they don't appear to fit the same social grouping as the others.

Reward

- Pay and terms of employment should not be based on age, but should reflect the value of individual contributions and standards of job performance;
- The National Minimum Wage (NMW) provisions will remain the same. The exemption linked to the NMW will allow employers using exactly the same age bands, i.e. 16 and 17, 18 to 21 and 22 and over, to pay at or above the national minimum rates provided those in the lower age group(s) are paid less than the adult minimum wage;
- You can still give benefits based on service if you can show that your use of length of service fulfils a business need (for example, by encouraging the loyalty, motivation or rewarding the experience of the workers). You would award the same benefit to anyone who came into that category;
- There are special provisions for calculating a worker's length of service for this purpose. On each occasion on which you decide to use the criterion of length of service in relation to an award, you must choose between two ways of calculating length of service. They are:
    - the length of time the worker has been working for you doing work which you reasonably consider to be at or

> above a certain level, assessed by reference to the demands made on the worker, or
> - the length of time the worker has been working for you in total;

- Benefits which accrue based on or below five years' service are exempt;
- You may have to do some research to show evidence that you do in fact increase loyalty, motivation etc. by giving these benefits.

Pensions

Occupational pension schemes are included by the legislation. Personal pensions not provided by the employer (except the employer's own contribution) are not covered by the regulations.

Employers will be able to provide different pension schemes to employees of different ages, or with different lengths of service and use minimum and maximum ages for admission to pension schemes and for the payment of pensions.

While the legislation makes it unlawful for the trustees and managers of occupational pension schemes to discriminate against members or prospective members on grounds of age, there are a number of exemptions. These include:

- Setting a minimum or maximum age for admission to the scheme;
- Setting a minimum level of pensionable pay for admission to a scheme provided that the level is not above the lower earnings limit;

- Setting a minimum age for payment for benefits provided that, in the case of benefits paid under a defined benefits arrangement before any early retirement pivot age, such benefits are subject to actuarial reduction and the member is not credited with added years;
- Only providing benefits to members who have completed more than a minimum period of service, provided that the minimum is not more than two years;
- In the case of money-purchase schemes, the use of different rates of employer or member contributions according to members' ages where this is done with the aim of equalising or making more equal the amount of benefit to which members of different ages in a comparable set of circumstances are entitled.

Training and development

- All employees should be eligible for training and development programmes. All age groups, even those near retirement, should be included;
- Give consideration to the way you deliver training and development. For example, it may be argued that online learning could discriminate against the older worker.

Retention and redundancy

- When releasing employees, the organisation's future needs for knowledge, skills and competencies should be taken into account. Alternatives to redundancy should be considered, such as shorter hours, part-time working or other contractual arrangements, secondments and perhaps employment breaks;

- When selecting for redundancy you should not automatically choose older workers;
- It's usual these days to put together a range of criteria for selection. They tend to include things like disciplinary record, attendance, skills, appraisal ratings etc. Avoid length of service as a criterion as it will be indirectly discriminatory.

Retirement

- Alternatives to retirement may be considered, such as shorter hours, part-time working, contractual arrangements, secondments and perhaps employment breaks;
- There is a misconception that workers can't retire before the age of 65. That's simply not so. A worker can retire before 65 if he wishes to do so. The law says that the worker cannot be required to retire before 65. There would have to be very compelling reasons to do so.

Disability Discrimination Act 1995

Before the Disability Discrimination Act came into force, disabled employees had to be registered disabled by a doctor and employers with 20 or more staff were supposed to have a disabled quota of 3% of their workforce. This was a voluntary code, so few employers met the standard.

Under the Disability Discrimination Act (DDA), "a person has a disability if he has a physical or mental impairment which has a substantial or long-term effect on his ability to carry out normal day-to-day activities". There is no definition of "impairment" in the Act, and previous case law has held that it must bear its ordinary and natural meaning. "Impairment" seems to be very widely interpreted. In one case, the Scottish Court of Session was asked to consider what is meant by an "impairment". The court ruled that it's possible to find that a person has a physical impairment without knowing what caused it and without finding the disabled person had any "illness".

The requirement for a mental impairment to be "clinically well recognised" was dropped when the Disability Discrimination Act 2005 came into force in December 2005. The change means that distinctions between whether an impairment is mental or physical are less important.

Some Examples Of Impairments

A disability can arise from a wide range of impairments. Very few conditions are automatically disabilities within the meaning of the DDA, but many are capable of being disabilities if all the elements of the definition are satisfied. All of the following have been found to be disabilities, based on the facts in the particular circumstances of the case:

- Sensory impairments, such as those affecting sight or hearing;
- Impairments with fluctuating or recurring effects such as rheumatoid arthritis, myalgic

encephalitis (me)/chronic fatigue syndrome (cfs), fibromyalgia, depression and epilepsy;
- Progressive illnesses, such as motor neurone disease, muscular dystrophy, forms of dementia and lupus;
- Organ specific illnesses, including respiratory conditions, such as asthma, and cardiovascular diseases, thrombosis, stroke and heart disease;
- Developmental conditions, such as autistic spectrum disorders (asd), dyslexia and dyspraxia;
- Learning difficulties;
- Mental health conditions and mental illnesses, such as depression, schizophrenia, eating disorders, bipolar affective disorders, obsessive compulsive disorders, as well as personality disorders and some self-harming behaviour;
- Illnesses produced by injury to the body or brain;
- Club foot;
- Back injury (soft back tissue);
- Photosensitive epilepsy;
- Cerebral palsy;
- Multiple sclerosis;
- Diabetes;
- Migrainous neuralgia.

Note that it may not always be possible to categorise a condition as either a physical or a mental impairment. The underlying cause of the impairment may be hard to establish and there may be adverse effects which are both physical and mental in nature. Furthermore, effects of a mainly physical nature may stem from an underlying mental impairment, and vice versa.

Causation of an impairment isn't relevant, even if the cause is a consequence of a condition which is excluded. For example, liver disease as a result of alcohol dependency would count as an impairment, although alcoholism itself is expressly excluded from the scope of the definition of disability in the DDA. What it is important to consider is the effect of the impairment, provided that it is not an excluded condition.

More Than One Medical Condition

In some cases an employee may have two or more medical conditions making it difficult to identify whether he is or is not disabled within the meaning of the law.

Example

Mr Butterfield was employed as a mechanical and electrical co-ordinator. His job required him to travel extensively by car. In November 2003, after a long day's driving, Mr Butterfield was so tired he stopped at a service area for a rest. Afterwards, he set off for home and exposed himself to two different groups of women having admitted that his head was full of "weird thoughts and emotions" at the time. He was subsequently convicted of indecent exposure and dangerous driving. The following day he attended a meeting at work and broke down and was later admitted to hospital for treatment. Mr Butterfield was diagnosed as suffering from a moderately severe depressive illness.

Mr Butterfield was advised by his solicitors that he did not have to disclose his convictions for indecent exposure to his employer. As a result, he told his employers that he was banned from driving and when questioned why police had quizzed him about a different matter he lied.

Eventually he told his employers the truth and was dismissed on the basis that he had misled them and his conduct could potentially bring the company into disrepute, as there was a risk that it may be repeated in the future.

Mr Butterfield brought a claim for discrimination based on his mental impairment. The tribunal found that his employer had treated him less favourably because of his condition on the basis that, had he not been suffering from the mental illness, he would not have committed the offences.

The employer successfully appealed. The EAT stated that it was clear that the sole reason for his dismissal related to his exhibitionism, a condition that did not amount to an impairment and that his dismissal did not relate to his depression, which is a qualifying impairment. The depression was underlying to an excluded condition (in this case the exhibitionism), that resulted in less favourable treatment. Therefore his disability (the depression) was not a reason for the less favourable treatment. Edmund Nuttall Limited v Butterfield [2005]

It is important to distinguish between an impairment that is regarded as a disability within the meaning of the DDA 1995 and an impairment that underlies an excluded condition under the 1996 Regulations. A tendency to steal, physical or sexual abuse of others and exhibitionism are some examples of conditions excluded from being treated as a disability and could potentially justify less favourable treatment. For the full list of excluded conditions, see page 93.

To impact "substantially", the condition must impact on an employee in a way which is more than minor or trivial. The exceptions are Multiple Sclerosis, HIV and most cancers which are now deemed to be disabilities from the time of diagnosis.

"Long term" isn't defined in the Act, but is widely taken to mean an illness or condition that is likely to last for 12 months or more, has lasted 12 months or more, is likely to last indefinitely or is episodic, for example, epilepsy or asthma. In other words, the underlying condition remains and the symptoms present from time to time.

When you are considering whether a condition is likely to be a disability or not, you have to ignore the corrective effects of medication (other than contact lenses or spectacles).

An impairment is to be taken to affect the ability of a person to carry out "normal day-to-day" activities only if it affects that person in respect of one or more of the following:

- Mobility;

- Manual dexterity;
- Physical co-ordination;
- Continence;
- Ability to lift, carry or otherwise move everyday objects;
- Speech, hearing or eyesight;
- Memory or ability to concentrate, learn or understand; or
- Perception of the risk of physical danger.

N.B. This list is <u>not</u> a list of day-to-day activities because it's not feasible to provide an exhaustive list, but they give a starting point for assessing the impact of a condition.

Day-to-day activities cover the things people do on a regular or daily basis. Guidance is given by the courts. Their examples include shopping, reading and writing, having a conversation or using the telephone, watching television, getting washed and dressed, preparing and eating food, carrying out household tasks, walking and travelling by various forms of transport, and taking part in social activities. Interestingly, sports and leisure pursuits are *not* included.

Example

Mr Shergill started work with Coca Cola Enterprises as a warehouseman in November 1999. As a result of an accident that he claimed that he suffered at work in December 1999, Mr Shergill was absent from work for almost a year. On 25th October 2000 he was dismissed on the grounds of incapability. He bought a claim before the employment tribunal that his dismissal amounted to disability discrimination.

In order to establish that he had a disability Mr Shergill gave examples of how his back condition impacted on his day-to-day activities citing cycling, keeping goal and playing snooker. The court found that was not sufficient to demonstrate a substantial adverse impact on normal day-to-day activities under the DDA. Sports, hobbies and games are not to be treated as normal day-to-day activities for the purposes of the Act. Coca Cola Enterprises v Shergill [2003]

Excluded Conditions

There are a number of conditions which are specifically excluded as disabilities. These are:

- Addiction to, or dependency on, alcohol, nicotine, or any other substance (other than the consequence of the substance being medically prescribed);
- Seasonal allergic rhinitis (for example, hay fever), except where it aggravates the effect of another condition;
- Tendency to set fires;
- Tendency to steal;
- Tendency to physical or sexual abuse of other persons;
- Exhibitionism;
- Voyeurism.

Despite the exception, recent cases have established that an employee may develop an illness or condition as a result of drug or alcohol addiction and this illness or condition may itself be a disability.

Example

Ms Power was employed as an area sales manager by Panasonic. In October 1997 she was signed off work sick with depression. She was drinking heavily at the time and remained off work until her dismissal in November 1998. It was not disputed that Ms Power was both depressed and drinking very heavily.

She complained that she had suffered disability discrimination. Panasonic argued that she had not been discriminated against because the depression had arisen from her alcoholic state, which while an illness, is specifically excluded as a disability. The EAT found that the depression, even if it was caused by the alcohol abuse, had a substantial and long-term adverse effect on her ability to carry out her normal day-to-day activities and she was suffering from a disability within the meaning of the Act. Power v Panasonic UK Ltd [2003]

Someone who is no longer disabled, but who met the requirements of the definition in the past, will still be covered by the Act. For example, a woman who experienced a mental illness that had a substantial and long-term adverse effect on her ability to carry out normal day-to-day activities four years ago, but who has experienced no recurrence of the condition, is still entitled to the protection afforded by DDA, as a person with a past disability.

Generalised "learning difficulties" can amount to a disability if they have an adverse effect on the employee's ability to carry out normal day to day activities, even if they do not amount to a clinically well recognised illness. There is no requirement that evidence of a disability must be provided by a doctor.

Example

Mr Dunham was employed by Ashford Windows Ltd as a fork lift truck driver in September 2002. He was dismissed in December 2002. He complained that his dismissal and Ashford Windows' failure to make reasonable adjustments amounted to disability discrimination.

The employer said that Mr Dunham did not have a clinically recognised mental illness amounting to "a mental impairment". They had done all they could, but he was unable to do his job in a safe manner and was therefore dismissed.

On appeal the EAT ruled that it was not necessary to establish a specific mental impairment or clinical condition for a person to suffer from a mental impairment within the meaning of the Act. It was clear that if the general learning difficulties are sufficiently serious they can amount to a mental impairment. Dunham v Ashford Windows[2005]

Knowledge Of A Disability

Where the disability is not obvious or you have no knowledge of it, can you be liable? Authorities are mixed but it seems you can be liable if the disability and worker's treatment are related.

Example

Mr Kenrick was absent from work on sick leave for a lengthy period. The cause, diagnosis and prognosis of his illness were unclear. Mr Kenrick told his manager he was due to see a specialist and asked the manager to wait for the result of that meeting before deciding whether or not to dismiss. The employer refused and dismissed him the next day. Shortly afterwards Mr Kenrick was diagnosed with Chronic Fatigue Syndrome. The court decided Mr Kenrick had been discriminated against even though the employer didn't know at the time that he had a disability. H J Heinz Co Ltd v Kenrick [2000]

Note that you may be expected to know about a person's disability by putting together certain relevant facts, even if the fact of the disability isn't specifically confirmed to you by the employee. Ensure that where information about potentially disabled employees comes though different channels there is a suitable and confidential process for bringing such information together. You can ask about disabilities as part of the recruitment process provided that you don't discriminate unjustifiably.

Example

Ms Hall suffered from a psychiatric condition which required her to take medication. Unfortunately, she wasn't taking it.

She was recruited by the Department for Work and Pensions (DWP). As part of the pre-employment process she filled out a health declaration form, but did not provide any information about disability or long-term health conditions. She refused to allow the DWP to contact her doctor.

Soon after starting employment she was involved in a series of incidents with other members of staff. She was issued with an oral warning that disciplinary action would follow unless she maintained the required standards of conduct.

At around the same time, Ms Hall applied for a disabled person's tax credit and asked her manager to sign the form, which he then sent to HR to process. A number of further incidents followed involving some verbal abuse and minor physical contact.

Ms Hall was taken through the disciplinary process and dismissed.

She argued that she had been less favourably treated for a reason relating to her disability. The employer's defence was that they hadn't been aware of her disability and thus could not have made reasonable adjustments.

The court said that the employer had constructive knowledge of her disability (that is, they were deemed to have knowledge) because Ms Hall's bizarre behaviour and the disability benefit form were arguably enough to put the employer on notice. It was no defence that Ms Hall had not expressly disclosed the information. In consequence the DWP was found to be in breach of their duties because it had not considered reasonable adjustments at all. Department of Work and Pensions v Hall [2005]

Discrimination occurs in two ways:

1. If for a reason related to the person's disability, you treat a disabled person less favourably than you treat or would treat other people, and cannot justify this treatment;
2. It also occurs when you fail to comply with a duty to make a reasonable adjustment in relation to the disabled person.

Reasonable Adjustments

As an employer you are under a duty to make reasonable adjustments to accommodate the needs of a disabled employee. A reasonable adjustment is any step or steps that you can reasonably take to ensure that existing workplace arrangements don't put the disabled person at a disadvantage in comparison with a non-disabled person.

While there is no specific duty laid upon you to consult with your employee about the adjustments, it will be a sensible course to take and one which a tribunal will expect.

Example

Mrs Tarling was dismissed due to her failure to meet production targets. She suffered from a club foot which caused her pain and discomfort at work where she was required to stand for long periods at a time.

The company sought advice regarding suitable chairs for her, and were told that she might be better able to do her job using a "Grahl" chair costing around £1000. The chair was available free of charge for a month's trial.

Instead of following this advice they simply dismissed her. The tribunal found that she had suffered unlawful discrimination because as the company had not followed the advice sought, they failed to make a reasonable adjustment.
Tarling v Wisdom Toothbrushes Limited [1997]

In 2004 the House of Lords went beyond what was previously considered a "reasonable adjustment".

Ms Archibald was a road sweeper for Fife Council. After surgery complications, she became virtually unable to walk. She retrained and unsuccessfully applied for over 100 sedentary office jobs with the council. Fife Council operated a competitive interviewing process and although Ms Archibald was qualified to apply, she was never the best candidate for the job. Eventually she was dismissed on grounds of capability. Ms Archibald's disability discrimination claim was unsuccessful at the employment tribunal, EAT and Court of Session, but she appealed successfully to the House of Lords. The House of Lords found that Ms Archibald was disadvantaged when compared with staff who were not disabled and there was a positive duty to make reasonable adjustments. It may have been reasonable for the council to automatically transfer her to an existing post at a slightly higher grade, for which she was qualified, even if she was not necessarily the best person for the job. Archibald v Fife Council [2004]

Examples of adjustments:

- Alteration of premises;
- Allocation of some duties to someone else;
- Transfer to another vacant job;
- Alteration of working hours;
- Changing the place of work;
- Supplying additional training;
- Acquiring or changing equipment;
- Allowing time off for treatment, including counselling.

Cost And Reasonable Adjustment

Generally cost will not be considered by the courts as sufficient good reason for failing to make an adjustment. The Code of Practice developed by the Disability Rights Commission provides us with some guidelines. Matters to be considered include:

- The practicability of the step;
- Financial and other costs of the adjustment and the extent of any disruption caused;
- The extent of the employer's financial or other resources;
- The availability to the employer of financial or other assistance to help make an adjustment.

Financial assistance can sometimes be made available. It's useful to talk to the DWP in the first instance for some guidance (www.dwp.gov.uk).

Amendments To The DDA

The original DDA has been added to several times and the amending legislation is summarised below.

The Disability (Blind and Partially Sighted Persons) Regulations 2003

These Regulations came into force in April 2003. People who have been certified as blind or partially sighted by a registered ophthalmologist or are registered as such with a local authority will automatically qualify for protection. Wearers of ordinary glasses and contact lenses are not covered!

Disability Discrimination Act 1995 (Amendment) Regulations 2003

This came into force in October 2004.

The main changes were:

- The introduction of a new definition of harassment;
- Prohibition of discrimination against contract workers;

- Post-employment discrimination became unlawful;
- Removal of the small employer exception. All employers must now comply with the requirements of the DDA;
- Shifting the burden of proof to the employer.

The Disability Discrimination Act 2005

This Act builds on and extends earlier disability discrimination legislation, principally the Disability Discrimination Act 1995.

Main provisions:

- It amended the definition of disability to automatically include HIV, most cancers and multiple sclerosis within its scope from the point of diagnosis;
- Removal of the requirement that mental illnesses no longer have to be clinically well recognised to afford protection under the DDA.

Actions for employers:

- Ensure that you keep open lines of communication between occupational health, HR and managers;
- Where an individual's behaviour is problematic (for whatever reason, for example, increased absenteeism or bizarre behaviour in the workplace) investigate it and give consideration as to whether or not the conduct at issue stems from some form of disability;
- When considering reasonable adjustments explore all the options with the employee and make notes, including what was discussed and rejected as well as what was agreed;
- Start from the point of what the employee *can* do rather than what he *can't* do;

- When assessing whether an employee has a disability, be aware that the individual may be afforded protection by the Act even if he cannot tell you what caused his condition and even if it doesn't appear that he suffers from an "illness" at all.

Equal Pay Act 1970

The equal pay legislation is designed to counteract inequalities in pay based upon sex discrimination. As a result, an equality clause is implied into any contract of employment.

Equal pay is not restricted to remuneration alone, but includes most terms of a contract of employment. Terms affording special treatment because of pregnancy or childbirth, or reflecting statutory restrictions on the employment of women are not covered.

The law requires you to pay the same in the following circumstances:

- If a woman is employed on like work with a man, that is, broadly similar, for example duties or hours; or
- She is employed on work rated as equivalent with that of a man, for example, effort, skills, decision making; or
- The work is of equal value i.e. that person must show reasonable grounds for claiming work of equal value.

Protection is given to both men and women under the Equal Pay Act, but in reality it tends to be women who are paid less than men and so they tend to make greater use of the legislation.

A woman is employed on "like work" with a man, if her work and his are of the same or a broadly similar nature, and any differences between the things they do are not of practical importance in relation to their terms and conditions of employment. It is for you to show the practical importance of any such differences as do exist.

If you can show that the difference in pay is genuinely explained by something that has nothing to do with gender the claim will fail.

If the defence is to succeed, you must prove that the factor:

- Existed at the date when the wages were fixed and/or the equal work commenced and then continued up to the date of the hearing;
- Is "material" i.e. that it is causally relevant and responsible for the difference in pay;
- Is "genuine" i.e. that it truly explains the difference in pay;
- Is not tainted by direct discrimination;
- If tainted by indirect discrimination, it can be justified on an objective basis.

An example of a material factor is where employees in their first six months of service are trainees and paid at a training rate. After the first six months the salary rate is increased. A woman in her first six months of service could not compare herself to a man doing the same job but who has more than six months service. The correct comparator would be a man in his first six months of service.

The Equal Pay Act was amended by new regulations in July 2003. Applicants can now claim six years back pay rather than two. However, if you have concealed information from an employee or the employee is a minor or of unsound mind the claim can date back as much as twenty years and the six month period after employment during which a claim must be brought can be extended.

The Employment Act 2002 gave employees the right to question you in an equal pay claim by means of a questionnaire. This procedure is intended to increase transparency in pay and reward systems, enabling employees and workers who believe they may be receiving unequal pay to establish the key facts before deciding whether or not to pursue a case to tribunal. Before this Act, you only had to disclose such information after proceedings had started.

If you fail to answer the questions or answer them in an evasive way, the tribunal may draw the inference that you are in breach of the Equal Pay Act.

Under these rules employees may:

- Request information on other named employees' pay, benefits and job function;
- Request a breakdown of earnings in particular jobs or roles;

- Seek information about pay schemes and job grading schemes;
- Seek an explanation of how you fix salary levels and annual increases;
- Ask whether any form of pay audit exists to ensure equality and fairness across pay structures.

Note that the use of a questionnaire will require you to get permission from a named employee to disclose his salary details. If the employee refuses to do that you still have to answer the questionnaire, but it will have to be in more general terms, so you may give the overall value of his remuneration package rather than details of salary and benefits.

Part Time Workers Regulations 2000

The aim of these Regulations is to ensure that part-time workers carrying out the same or broadly similar activities as those carried out by comparable full-time workers are treated no less favourably in their working conditions, unless the less favourable treatment is justified on objective business grounds.

For the purposes of these regulations "workers" includes employees and workers i.e. temps, casuals and agency staff.

This means they should:

- Receive the same rates of pay (including overtime pay, once they have worked more than the normal full-time hours);

- Not be treated less favourably for contractual sick pay or maternity pay purposes, or discriminated against over access to pension schemes or pension scheme benefits;
- Not be excluded from training simply because they work part-time;
- Receive holiday entitlement *pro rata* to that of comparable full-timers;
- Have career break schemes, contractual maternity leave and parental leave made available to them in the same way as for full-time employees;
- Be treated no less favourably in the criteria for selection for redundancy.

Example

In January 2001 Hendrickson told Ms Pipe, a part time worker, that if she wished to remain in employment she would have to extend her working hours to full-time as it had decided to reduce the number of accounting assistants to three full-time employees. Ms Pipe had three other colleagues performing the same job. They all worked full-time and none them had been employed by the company for more than a few months. Ms Pipe offered to increase her hours to 32.5 hours per week (only five hours less than the full-time workers) but was unable to agree to work full time because of personal commitments. She was subsequently made redundant and complained to tribunal that she had been selected for redundancy because of her part-time status.

The tribunal found that the company had unfairly dismissed Ms Pipe and that she had been treated less favourably than a comparable full-time employee on the basis of her part-time status. She was awarded £50,550 as a compensatory award. Hendrickson Europe Limited v Pipe [2003]

The issue of the "same or broadly similar" activities was considered by the House of Lords in a test case brought by retained (part-time) fire fighters alleging they had been less favourably treated than the full-time firefighters.

Example

A number of retained fire fighters claimed unlawful discrimination by being denied access to the Fireman's Pension Scheme, arrangements for sick pay and increased pay for additional responsibilities. The Court of Appeal rejected their claim. Although the retained and full-time firefighters were employed under the same type of contract for the purposes of the regulations, they did not do the "same or broadly similar work".

The House of Lords allowed the appeal. They looked at the work done by both groups as a whole, considering similarities and differences and said that the question is not whether it is different, but whether it is broadly similar. The extent to which the work that they do is exactly the same is vital. In this case the work was found to be broadly similar. Matthews v Kent & Medway Town Fire Authority [2006]

Actions for employers:

- When comparing jobs look at the work done by both groups as a whole and consider similarities and differences. The question is not whether it is different, but whether it is broadly similar;
- Be careful if you have a situation where full and part-time workers do the same work, but the full-timers have extra activities which fill their time. This will not necessarily prevent their work being the same or broadly similar overall;
- When comparing roles, you need to give particular weight to the extent to which the full- and part-time work is in fact the same, and to the importance of that work to your organisation. If you fail to do that, you risk giving too much weight to differences which are the inevitable result of one worker working full-time and another working less than full-time.

Trade Union Membership

Every employee has the right to belong to a trade union, or not to belong to a trade union if he so chooses. It is unlawful to discriminate against a person on the grounds of his membership of a trade union.

Chapter 3

Contracts Of Employment

20. Why Do We Need A Contract Of Employment?

You must give employees a written statement of the main particulars of their employment within two months of the start of their employment. The statement should include details of pay, hours, holidays, notice period and disciplinary and grievance procedures. Most employers refer to this written statement as the contract. In fact it only forms part of the contract, which may be made up of a number of documents (such as the offer letter) or other verbal arrangements.

Small employers should note that there is no exemption from the unfair dismissal rules. Where they don't have a disciplinary procedure, the statutory procedures form the minimum legal requirement. However, it is sensible to have a fuller disciplinary procedure and clear rules in place because it clarifies standards and expectations and clearly indicates the consequences in the event of a breach.

Employees who are not provided with a written statement of employment particulars by their employer, or who are not notified of a change in those particulars, or who contest the accuracy of the written statement, may refer the matter to an employment tribunal. The Employment Act 2002 empowers employment tribunals to award compensation to employees who have not received written statements, or whose written statements are incomplete.

21. What Must Be Included In The Written Particulars?

The list of matters to be covered by the written particulars is laid out in the ERA 1996. They are as follows:

- Names of the parties to the contract;
- Dates;
- Remuneration and the date at which it is to be paid;
- Hours, including overtime arrangements;
- Holidays;
- Job title or brief job description;
- The period for which the contract is expected to continue, i.e., permanent or for a fixed term;
- Place of work;
- Sick pay rules;
- Pensions;
- Notice;
- Collective agreements;
- Working abroad;
- Discipline and grievance procedures.

It is open to you to add your own requirements to the list. For example, you may want to add rules relating to dress code or personal mobile phone usage during business hours.

22. Who Is An Employee?

Employees and employers have various rights, duties, obligations and liabilities under a contract of employment.

As the employer you are bound by the terms of the contract of employment and may be vicariously liable for your employee's actions in the course of his employment. You must deduct income tax and National Insurance from the employee's wages and you have duties in relation to health and safety and unlawful discrimination.

Employees are people who have an employment contract and are bound by its terms. They have to carry out their work duties in person. Employees have a range of rights that are not available to workers or the self-employed. Section Four describes the rights of employees and workers.

Statutory employment rights are minimum terms. For example, the law gives a right to a minimum amount of paid holiday. You can give an enhanced contractual holiday entitlement if you choose, and many employers do (though you cannot give less than the statutory minimum). You and your employee are free to agree better terms between yourselves in a contract of employment or collective agreement. When the terms of a contract of employment are broken, either party may have grounds to make a complaint of breach of contract to the tribunal or court.

23. Workers And The Self-Employed

A worker is a person such as a casual or a temp supplied by an agency. Self-employed people may be sole traders or trade in limited companies. Workers and the self-employed don't have a contract of employment with you. They may be working under some sort of contract it isn't an employment contract. One of the key points in deciding whether or not there is an employment relationship is the degree of control exercised by you and whether there is mutuality of obligation.

Mutuality of obligation means you both each other a duty. Your obligation is to provide work for a worker. The worker's obligation is to attend and do the work. If the opposite applies, i.e. that there is no obligation upon you to provide work and there is no obligation upon the worker to carry out the work, in that case there is unlikely to be an employment relationship. In these circumstances, you must make it clear to the worker that there is no intention to create an employment relationship.

Workers

Workers may work on a casual, wages-only agreement, where they are paid only for the hours they work and do not assume any other employment rights. Employers using temps or casuals will often assume responsibility for deducting tax and National Insurance. This is an administrative convenience and does not of itself means that the worker is employed.

Like employees, workers carry out the work in person and cannot use a substitute.

However, if such employment continues for a long time, a worker may acquire continuity of employment and be deemed to be an employee. This will give him many additional rights:

If you use casual workers, make sure you do the following.

- Clarify their employment status;
- Explain the duration (or expected duration) of the employment period;
- Establish what rights they will acquire if employment continues.

Until a couple of years ago, it was thought very unlikely that agency workers could properly be classified as employees of the end-users of their services because there would not usually be any express contract in place between an agency worker and the end-user.

A series of cases have challenged that belief. In *Brook Street Bureau (UK) Ltd v Dacas [2004]* the Court of Appeal held that Mrs Dacas, an agency worker, was not an employee of the employment business that supplied her. They found that in certain circumstances an implied contract of employment could arise between an agency worker and the end user client.

Example

Mrs Dacas worked for over four years as a cleaner at a site owned by Wandsworth Council. Wandsworth Council had a contract with Brook Street for the supply of Mrs Dacas' services. The contracts between Mrs Dacas and Brook Street and in turn between Brook Street and Wandsworth Council (the "end user") were typical temporary worker contracts, with Brook Street retaining responsibility for paying Mrs Dacas and for matters such as discipline, holidays and sick pay. In practice Mrs Dacas was under the control of Wandsworth Council in respect of her hours of work and what she did hour by hour during a working day. The contracts were framed in a way that (so far as Brook Street was concerned) did not create "mutuality of obligation" between Mrs Dacas and any other person for employment rights purposes.

An incident occurred after which Wandsworth Council asked Brook Street to remove Mrs Dacas. Mrs Dacas claimed that she had been unfairly dismissed by Brook Street or Wandsworth Council. Only an employee can claim unfair dismissal so Mrs Dacas had first to establish that she was an employee.

The court looked beyond the written terms of those contracts and considered whether there was an implied contract of employment between the worker and the end user. In drawing their conclusion they made some interesting comments. Such comments are not binding but they help us understand the court's approach. One comment was that the end user will often have enough power of control or direction over the worker to be the worker's employer. Another point made was that it was not credible that a worker in these circumstances was employed by neither the end user nor the agency. Finally, once a worker had been working for the same end user for one year or more, the court said it could be inferred in some cases that a contract of employment had been created.

The decision in Dacas was followed in *Cable & Wireless v Muscat [2006].*

Mr Muscat was employed by Cable & Wireless, although payments were made to his service company, E-Nuff. Cable & Wireless told Mr Muscat that in future it wanted him to provide his services through an agency, Abraxas, which already had a contract to supply personnel to the company.

A separate contract was then entered into between E-Nuff and Abraxas for the supply of Mr Muscat's services to Cable & Wireless, and Mr Muscat continued working as before under the direction of Cable & Wireless. His only contact with Abraxas was in relation to the payment of his invoices.

In December 2002, Mr Muscat's contract was terminated and he complained that he had been unfairly dismissed. In light of the Dacas decision, the tribunal considering his unfair dismissal claim was satisfied that there was an implied contract between Mr Muscat and Cable & Wireless. Cable & Wireless appealed.

Significantly, the court accepted that no contract could be implied unless it was deemed as necessary to give business reality to a transaction.

On the facts of the Muscat case, the CA held that there was an implied contract, because before Mr Muscat entered into the arrangement with the agency he was already in an employment relationship with the end-user. That employment contract was not terminated when he entered into the contract with the agency. The only thing that had changed was the arrangement for payment.

This case is authority for the proposition that an implied contract can only exist in certain circumstances. In order for an employment contract to exist there must be:

- Mutuality of obligation (on the employer to provide work and pay and on the employee to accept and perform services personally);
- Employer control over the employee;
- Relationships consistent with employment (for example. provision of equipment, employee-type benefits and integration into the business).

Note that most agency workers will not be in an existing employment relationship with the end-user before converting to agency status.

Determining Employment Status

There is no one thing that completely determines a worker's employment status. If there is a dispute about the status between a worker and employer, all the circumstances of a case will be considered.

The sort of things the tribunal look at fall into four main categories. Below are some questions to help explain what the categories mean.

The more questions being answered "yes", the more likely it is that the worker is self-employed. If more questions are answered "no", the more likely the worker is to be an employee.

This is for guidance only and a definitive answer can only be given by an employment tribunal or court.

The four main categories and associated questions are:

Control. To what extent do you decide what tasks the worker does and how he does them?

- Does the worker have the final say in how the business is run?
- Can the worker choose whether to do the work himself, or send someone else to do it?
- Can the worker choose when and how he will work?

Integration. To what extent is the worker part of the organisation?

- If the worker needs assistance, is he responsible for hiring other people and setting their terms of employment?
- Is the worker excluded from internal company matters such as corporate training and staff meetings?
- Is the worker exempt from having action taken against him using the company disciplinary procedure?
- Is the worker excluded from company benefits and pension schemes?

Mutuality of obligation. To what extent are you required to offer the worker work? To what extent is the worker is required to do that work?

- Does your company offer work only if and when it is available?
- Can the worker decide when he will work and can he turn down work when it is offered?

Economic reality. How much financial risk does the worker bear?

- Is the worker responsible for meeting the losses as well as taking the profits?
- Is the worker responsible for correcting unsatisfactory work at his own expense?
- Does the worker have to submit an invoice to the company in order to receive payment?
- Does the worker get a fixed payment for a job (including materials and labour)?
- Does the worker provide the main items of equipment needed to do the job?

- Does the worker work for a range of different employers?

Actions for employers:

- Review the commercial basis for engaging agency workers. Is it still valid?
- Only use agency workers for short term assignments;
- If you have agency workers on long term assignments, consider transferring them to employed status;
- Deal with agencies rather than the worker over discipline, holiday and control of work;
- In so far as it is consistent with discrimination legislation, treat agency workers differently to the permanent workforce;
- Check that there is adequate indemnity protection in any agency contract against the risk of claims and that documentation reflects the commercial reality of the relationship.

24. Modern Apprentices

A modern apprenticeship can be treated like a traditional one. This has implications for the amount of compensation payable if an apprentice is dismissed.

Example

Seventeen year old Mr Flett started an apprenticeship in September 2002 under the electrical industry's modern apprenticeship training plan. Under this apprenticeship he worked for Matheson and had time off to be trained by a training provider, with the intention of becoming a qualified electrician.

He was dismissed without notice before his training was complete and made a claim to an employment tribunal arguing that if he had become a qualified electrician he would have been earning good money. Taking account of what he would have earned if the apprenticeship had continued for the full term, Mr Flett's losses by not qualifying amounted to £50,000.

Matheson argued that Mr Flett was an employee and as a result was only entitled to claim for the week's notice that he should have been given.

Under a traditional apprenticeship, if an employer fails to provide training, the apprentice is entitled to be paid for the outstanding part of the contract and to get damages for the lack of qualification and reduced earnings. For example, an employer can't make an apprentice redundant without breaching the contract.

Since the agreement required Mr Flett to work for Matheson as an apprentice while earning wages from them and training for a period of considerable length with their support to qualify as an electrician, the agreement had the essential features of a contract of apprenticeship. Under the agreement, if continuation of the arrangement did not suit the circumstances of the employer, Matheson had to try to find an alternative employer. If such attempts failed, the obligation remained on the company and they could not dismiss the apprentice within the period of training, save in cases of incapability. As various terms of the arrangement had been insufficiently explored, the matter was remitted to the employment tribunal for further consideration of the evidence. Flett v Matheson [2006]

25. Variation Of Contract

A contract may be varied by:

- Mutual agreement between the employee and employer;
- Collective agreement with a recognised trade union;
- Use of a flexibility clause;
- Statute;
- Dismissal and re-engagement;
- Custom and practice.

If you unilaterally impose a change to a contract and the change is not accepted, the variation will constitute a breach and could lead to a claim for constructive dismissal. In order to reduce the risk of a claim you should consult with affected employees and try to remove or reduce their objections before making changes to the contract.

Mutual Agreement

Most changes take place by mutual consent. The most common example of an agreed change is an increase in salary. It is always sensible to obtain express agreement i.e. written evidence that the employee has agreed to the change.

In some cases agreement can be implied if you propose a change and your employee carries out the job under the changed conditions without complaint. However, there can be problems with this situation, especially where the terms are not immediately effective. It is always best to try and obtain written agreement.

Example

Mrs Aparau was employed as a cashier for Bejams in Tottenham in north London. On a number of occasions she had voluntarily agreed to work at other Bejams shops nearby. Bejams was taken over by Iceland. Following the takeover Iceland issued all staff with new written terms and conditions, which included a mobility clause. Mrs Aparau expressed concern about the new terms but didn't follow it through formally. After about 18 months working at Tottenham, there was a disagreement between Mrs Aparau and her supervisor and Mrs Aparau was told she would have to work at an Iceland shop nearby. She refused to do so and when her manager tried to enforce the instruction, she resigned and claimed unfair dismissal through the constructive dismissal route.

Iceland tried to rely on Mrs Aparau's failure to object to the mobility clause and argued that after 18 months it was now part of the contract. As the term had not been tested until the day Iceland asked her to move, the court found that mere continuance of employment without objection could not be taken to indicate acceptance. Aparau v Iceland Frozen Foods [1996]

Collective Agreement

Where you negotiate with a recognised union or other body representing workforce interests, the variation could become incorporated within the individual contract of employment either by an express provision, by implication or custom and practice. The outcome of collective agreements can be expressly incorporated into contracts and this is achieved by inserting wording which indicates that employees are employed on the basis of any national or local agreements currently in force.

Flexibility Clause

Some contracts of employment contain a clause which gives you the right to vary the terms of the contract. They may relate to, for example, an employee's rate of pay, to his working hours, place or conditions of employment.

Note his does <u>not</u> give you the right to make unilateral changes. Even with a flexibility clause, the changes are confined to those of a minor, non-fundamental type.

Statute

If legislation is passed where the statutory benefits or requirements exceed those conferred by the existing contract, the new statutory terms will automatically replace the contractual terms. An example is the National Minimum Wage Act 1998 which gives employees and workers the right to a minimum hourly rate of pay.

Dismissal And Re-Engagement

This applies where the new terms have not been agreed and change can only be achieved by serving notice to terminate the existing contract and offering to re-engage the employee on different terms. Try to change a contract by some other method before taking this option. This is the last resort as there is the strong possibility of an unfair dismissal claim.

Example

In the early 1980s Rupert Murdock wanted to move his newspaper print works from Fleet Street to Wapping. The workforce was still heavily unionised and refused to move voluntarily, so he dismissed them and recruited new staff. They picketed the new works for months and it was an acrimonious and highly public dispute.

Custom And Practice

Some terms and conditions of employment become established because they have been the way of doing things for a long period of time. They are unwritten practices, but rapidly become accepted, for example, early work finish on Fridays. Where such customs have grown up, changing them suddenly, without due notice and consultation, may lead to successful claims for constructive dismissal.

Customs must be reasonable, certain and well known. It will only be implied by custom if there is nothing in the express or necessarily implied terms of the contract to prevent such inclusion.

26. Confirming Changes To The Contract

A contractual change must be confirmed in writing within four weeks of the date of variation. You don't need to reissue the whole set of terms and conditions again, only the part of the contract that has been changed.

Chapter 4

Employment Rights

27. Genuinely Self-Employed

The general rule is that employees, workers and self-employed people have the right not to suffer from unlawful discrimination on grounds of race, sex, (including gender reassignment), disability, religious belief, sexual orientation, their status as a part time worker or age.

They further share the right to:

- Equal pay for equal work, for work of equal value or work rated as equivalent;
- Belong or not to belong to a trade union and to take part in trade union activities;
- Work in reasonable safety.

28. Rights Of Workers

As well as the rights listed above, employees and workers have the right to:

- Four weeks' paid holidays. Four weeks is based on the number of days or hours that an employee works. So, for example, if an employee is contracted to work four days a week, he will have 16 days holiday;
- A maximum working week of 48 hours on average and the right to have weekly and daily rest breaks;
- Receive the National Minimum Wage;
- Be accompanied at a disciplinary or grievance hearing.

They also have a right to protection:

- Under the Public Interest Disclosure Act 1998 ("whistleblowing");
- Against unlawful deductions from wages.

Workers who fulfil the requirements will also qualify for Statutory Sick Pay.

29. Paid Holidays And Hours of Work

The Working Time Regulations 1998 provide some rights and protections as follows:

- A limit of an average of 48 hours a week which a worker can be required to work (though workers can choose to work more if they want to);
- The average week is calculated against a 17 week reference period;
- A limit of an average of eight hours work in 24 for night workers;
- A right for night workers to receive free health assessments;
- A right to 11 hours rest a day;
- A right to a day off each week or two days per fortnight;
- A right to a 20 minute rest break if the working day is longer than six hours. This may be paid or unpaid;
- A right to four weeks' paid leave per year (starting from day one at work).

Working Time

Example

In the case of Landeshauptstadt v Jaeger [2003] it was confirmed that if a worker is on call while at work (even if there is provision for him to sleep during the periods he is not needed) the on call time is classified as working time.

The principle has been extended to cover employees with homes on an employer's site. Ms McCartney worked four days on and three days off, but after she completed her work she was on call in her flat. The court decided she was working for the whole of the time she was on call, as well as the four days she actually worked. McCartney v Oversley House Management [2006]

Changes to the definition of working time came into force in April 2006. Currently there is a 48 hour weekly limit on working time averaged over a 17 week reference period. When calculating working time the following must be included:

- Predetermined working time. For example, an employee's contract of employment might require him to work 39 hours per week;
- Time where a worker is expressly required to work, for example, attendance at meetings;
- Time a worker is implicitly required to attend for work for example because of the requirements for the job.

From 6th April 2006 all of the worker's working time counts towards the 48 hour maximum and night working restrictions. Any hours worked either voluntarily or because they are required must be included when considering maximum working time limits and night work hours.

Actions for employers:

- Ensure that employees work a maximum of 48 hours;

- If employees regularly work more than 48 hours, despite what is written in their contract and they have not signed an opt-out, you must ensure that either the 48 hour maximum is observed or that the signed opt-out agreements are in place.

Taking Holiday Leave

In the UK it is not permissible to make a payment in lieu of untaken statutory holiday entitlement, except on the termination of employment, nor is there provision for workers to carry forward holiday which has not been taken in the current holiday year. The ECJ has now given a rather surprising decision that employees who do not take all their annual leave within a given year must be allowed to carry their minimum holiday entitlement to the next year.

In Federatie Nederlandse Vakbeweging v Staat der Nederlanden [2006] the ECJ noted that the positive effects on a worker's health and safety are maximised where holiday is taken in the current leave year. That benefit could still remain if the leave was taken in a subsequent holiday year. But while it was not contrary to the Directive to carry the leave over, the possibility of financial settlement for carried-over leave created an incentive for the leave to remain untaken, and was incompatible with its health and safety objectives.

It remains to be seen if the UK Government decides whether to follow this ruling. In the meantime, while national law says that we must not allow statutory holiday to be carried forward, it will be best to avoid this as a regular policy. Contractual holiday which exceeds statutory holiday can be carried forward quite lawfully.

Even contractual holiday should only be carried forward in exceptional circumstances, not every year. It should be limited to a maximum, for example, of a week or ten days.

Tip: Encourage your employees to plan and take their holiday entitlement in the year in which it arises.

Holiday Pay

The Working Time Regulations 1998 provides that workers are entitled to four weeks' paid annual leave. The question of whether a sick employee continues to accrue holiday pay was considered in Commissioners of Inland Revenue v Ainsworth [2005]. Mr Ainsworth was absent from work on long-term sick leave. He brought a claim seeking to establish that his entitlement to paid holiday under the Regulations continued even while he was not attending work. The claim was based on the EAT's earlier judgement in Kigass Aero Components Ltd v Brown [2002]. In the Kigass case the EAT allowed Mr Brown, who had been absent from work on long term sick leave, to claim holidays accruing during his period of sickness absence.

The Court of Appeal agreed with the Inland Revenue's argument that "leave" connotes a release from what would otherwise be an obligation. It would be contrary to all ordinary usage for a worker who is off work for a year or more, as a result of serious illness, to say that during some arbitrarily chosen part of that period he is taking "leave". Further, the Regulations are intended to ensure minimum health and safety standards in relation to working time, so that workers can expect a minimum period of release from the pressures of work. An interpretation along the lines proposed by the claimants would do nothing to further the interests of health and safety. The only result would be a windfall for the claimant. Mr Ainsworth was unsuccessful with his claim.

The Court also overturned the EAT's decision in List Design v Douglas [2002]. In this case, the employees were able to claim that non-payment of holiday pay amounted to an unlawful deduction from wages. They cited the Employment Rights Act 1996 which allows claims to be brought within three months of the last in a series of deductions. The Working Time Regulations state that claims must be brought within three months of the initial breach of the right to annual leave.

The court agreed that Mr Ainsworth should not be able to claim for backdated holiday pay over a period of several years. Under the WTR, employees can only claim for unpaid statutory holiday entitlement for the year in which that entitlement falls, and claims should be brought within three months of the date on which the right arises.

Calculation Of Holiday Pay

There are several different ways of calculating holiday pay.

If an employee's pay for work done in normal working hours does not vary, a week's pay will be the pay due for the basic hours the employee is contracted to work. Any regular bonus or allowance (except an expense allowance) which does not vary with the amount of work done may be included.

If an employee's pay varies with the amount of work done as, for example, under piece-work systems, or when pay is partly made up of variable bonuses or commission related to output performance, then a week's pay for normal working hours (excluding overtime hours not binding on both sides, as above) is based on a specially calculated hourly rate. This rate is the average hourly rate over a 12-week period, ending on the calculation date, if the calculation date is the last day of the pay week. If the calculation date falls during a pay week, the 12-week period ends on the last day of the previous week. To get this special average hourly rate, only hours when the employee was working (including overtime hours) can be taken into account.

If, at the calculation date, an employee is contracted to work normal hours, but on days of the week or at times of the day which differ from week to week, or over a longer time so that the pay for any week varies, (for example when the normal hours worked at night or at the weekend attract a higher rate of pay), then a week's pay means pay for the average number of normal weekly working hours at the average hourly rate.

To allow for variation of hours according to the shift worked, the average number of normal weekly working hours is calculated by dividing by 12 the total number of normal working hours during a period of 12 weeks, ending on the calculation date if the calculation date is the last day of the pay week. If the calculation date falls during a pay week, the 12-week period ends on the last day of the previous pay week. The average hourly rate is worked out in the same way as for piece-workers,

There has been considerable debate about the calculation of holiday pay where an employee regularly works and is paid for overtime.

Example

The Court of Appeal considered the case of Mr Bamsey, who was contracted to work 39 hours a week but who averaged a 58 hour week with overtime.

Overtime was compulsory but not guaranteed. (Guaranteed overtime means that the worker will be paid the overtime irrespective of whether he works it.) Mr Bamsey claimed that his holiday pay should be based on his average weekly pay, including overtime, as to find otherwise, would be contrary to the intention of the Working Time Regulations and would deter workers in his position from taking annual leave.

The Court considered the definition of a week's pay and found that it does not include overtime unless the overtime is both compulsory and guaranteed by the employer. Holiday pay would be calculated based on his weekly contractual hours.
Bamsey v Albon Engineering [2004]

Rolled-Up Holiday Pay

Rolled-up holiday pay is holiday pay that is paid as part of the hourly or weekly rate throughout the year and not paid separately at the time the holiday is taken. Debate has raged over this and a situation arose where in Scotland rolled-up holiday pay was unlawful, but in England it could be lawful in certain circumstances. The whole thing was referred to the ECJ who has now ruled that rolled-up holiday pay is, unlawful.

In its decision the ECJ ruled:

- You cannot simply allocate part of an existing wage packet to holiday pay. The holiday pay must be an *additional* payment to that made in respect of work actually done;
- You *must* pay holiday pay during the specific period during which the worker takes leave. It is unlawful to stagger payment over the year;
- But if you do roll-up extra money in respect of holiday pay, you can set-off the extra money already paid against the payments it ought to make during the specific holiday period. The burden is on you to prove the transparency of the payment.

The DTI has amended its guidance to reflect this decision and advises employers to renegotiate contracts involving holiday pay for existing workers as soon as possible, so that statutory holiday pay is paid at the time the holiday is actually taken. Although the ECJ found that rolled up holiday pay is unlawful, the DTI believes that the judgement allows for the offset of payments already made until the practice is discontinued. It states that payment already made for work undertaken can be offset against any future leave payments made at the proper time, provided that these payments are made in a transparent and comprehensible manner.

Daily Rest Breaks

Workers working for longer than six hours a day are entitled to a daily rest break which may be paid or unpaid. In the absence of a collective agreement this break period must be a minimum of 20 minutes.

There are some exemptions. These apply where "the worker's activities involve the need for continuity of service or production" or "where there is a foreseeable surge of activity".

There are few cases in this area but some guidance was offered in *Gallagher and Ors v Alpha Catering Services Ltd [2005]*. The court had to decide whether these exemptions applied to Mr Gallagher and his colleagues, whose job it was to deliver to and unload in-flight catering supplies and equipment to and from the aircraft they were servicing.

Mr Gallagher and his colleagues would often experience periods of downtime, when they would have to wait with their delivery vehicles for further instructions. However, when loading and unloading the aircraft they were working under strict time-limits which, if breached, could result in the employer incurring financial penalties. During the period in question there had been an increase in the number of flights Mr Gallagher and his colleagues were dealing with from 800 to 1,100 per week.

The court found that the exemptions didn't apply here. The need for continuity of service in this case applied not to the workers' activities, but to the needs of the employer's business. It noted that if this were the determining factor, unscrupulous employers may deliberately under-staff their work force in order to artificially create a business need for the removal of rest breaks. It further held that the second exemption properly applies in the context of foreseeable periodical or seasonal surges where there is an exceptional increase in activity. These requirements were not met in the instant case. The downtime experienced by Mr Gallagher was working time. They were effectively carrying out their duties by being continually available for work during this period.

The DTI's guidance about taking breaks says that an employer must make sure that his staff can take their rest, but he is not required to make sure they do take their rest.

In Commission of the European Communities v United Kingdom [2006] the European Commission challenged the DTI's guidelines, arguing that they "endorse and encourage a practice of non-compliance with the requirements of the directive".

The ECJ agreed that the UK had failed to meet its obligations under the directive. In letting it be understood that employers were under no obligation to ensure that workers actually exercised their rights, the guidelines were liable to render those rights meaningless, it said. It did acknowledge, however, that as a general rule, employers need not force their workers to claim the rest periods due to them.

As a result of this case, it is likely that you will have to put in place policies to ensure that workers take their breaks, encourage workers to observe the minimum rest periods and ensure that rest breaks are scheduled. Set out workers' entitlements to breaks in written policies, emphasising that the breaks must be taken.

An employer who does not inform his workers of the right to breaks and fails to put in place systems making sure that breaks are taken will be in breach of the regulations.

The Road Transport (Working Time) Regulations 2005

The Road Transport Regulations came into force in April 2005. Under the WTR mobile workers in the road transport sector have limited rights. These are a right to four weeks' paid annual leave and a right to health assessments for night workers. The Road Transport Regulations provide additional rights in relation to a maximum weekly working time, night work and rest and break provisions.

The genuinely self-employed are excluded from the provisions of the WTR until March 2009. However, the definition of 'self-employed' under the

Regulations is narrower than that used for the purposes of other legislation. The amount of control that a driver has over his work and his reliance on profits for an income is key. Where an individual's ability to work for another client is restricted, he will be covered by the Road Transport Regulations.

There are some workers who mainly carry out other work, for example, warehouse work, but on occasion are required to carry out work that comes under the provisions of the EU Drivers' Hours Rules. They are known as "occasional mobile workers". The EU Drivers' Hours Rules applies to these workers as appropriate. In their usual roles they are not covered by the Regulations, but by the WTR.

An occasional mobile worker is someone who works less than 11 days under the EU Drivers' Hours Rules in a reference period of less than 26 weeks, or less than 16 days in a reference period of 26 weeks or longer.

If a worker is not carrying out any other work as a member of the travelling crew, his time does not come within the definition of working time as set out in the Regulations. The time spent travelling with the driver is a "period of availability" and excluded from any calculation of working time. As long as the worker is not carrying out any other work, this period could count towards his break entitlement. However, if the worker is carrying out some other work, for example, if he is navigating the route for the driver, then this will be considered to be working time.

Where a worker is paid by and has a contractual

relationship with an employment business, that business is responsible for monitoring and keeping the relevant records as required by the Regulations. Where the worker is employed via an employment agency, but is paid by and has a contractual relationship with the hirer, that responsibility will rest with the hirer.

As with the WTR you have to decide in advance what method will be used for calculating and monitoring working time. Many employers choose to use the 17-week rolling reference period already used under the WTR. Some prefer to use an agreed fixed reference period up to a maximum of 26 weeks.

If you wish to use individual agreements to determine reference periods in advance, where there are part-time workers for example, you should bear in mind that the maximum length of a reference period allowed under these arrangements is 18 weeks.

You must keep records to show that the weekly working time and night-time work limits are being complied with, and monitor working time to ensure that the 48-hour average weekly limit is not exceeded. The Regulations do not specify exactly what form the records should take, but they must be adequate for the purpose for which they are required.

30. The National Minimum Wage Act 1998

The National Minimum Wage 1998 was introduced in 1999 and applies to nearly all workers.

Under this legislation, workers are entitled to be paid at least the level of the statutory National Minimum Wage (NMW) for every hour they have worked for an employer. The rates set are based on the recommendations of the independent Low Pay Commission.

There are different minimum wage rates for different groups of workers as follows:

- The main rate for workers aged 22 and over;
- The development rate for 18-21 year olds;
- The development rate for 16-17 year olds.

The age discrimination legislation does not affect the NMW.

What Is Pay?

As well as a worker's basic pay, there are other elements of pay which may count towards the NMW hourly rate. These include incentives such as merit or performance-related pay and bonuses.

Extra money above basic pay (for example, overtime or shift work premiums) does not count. Regional allowances which are not included in an employee's basic pay do not count. All benefits in kind (benefits other than money), except accommodation, do not count.

145

What Counts As Hours?

The number of hours for which workers must be paid the National Minimum Wage is worked out according to the type of work they do. There are four different types of work:

- Time work: the number of hours or period of time is set by you. You must pay workers at least the NMW in each pay period (usually the period of time for which a worker's wage is actually worked out), but you may take account of different hours worked in different periods;
- Salaried-hours work: a contract to work a set number of basic hours each year with a yearly salary paid in equal instalments. You must pay workers at least the NMW in each pay period;
- Output work: workers are paid purely according to their productivity, for example, how many products they produce or their sales. You may make an agreement, in writing, with a worker that gives a 'fair estimate' of the number of hours he will work. If you do not make an agreement, you must pay the worker at least the NMW for the hours he actually works;
- Unmeasured work: for workers where there are no set hours or measures of their output. You may make an agreement, in writing, with a worker that estimates the average number of hours they will work each day. If you do not make an agreement, you must pay the worker at least the NMW for the hours he actually works.

31. The Public Interest Disclosure Act 1998

The Act provides protection for "whistleblowers". These are workers who are dismissed or victimised as a result of making a qualifying disclosure.

The disclosure must, in the reasonable belief of the worker making the disclosure, show one of the following:

- That a criminal offence has been committed, is being committed or is likely to be committed;
- That a person has failed, is failing or is likely to fail to comply with any legal obligation to which he is subject;
- That a miscarriage of justice has occurred, is occurring or is likely to occur
- That the health and safety of the individual has been, is being or is likely to be endangered;
- That the environment has been, is being or is likely to be endangered;
- That information tending to show any matter falling within one of the above paragraphs has been, is being or is likely to be concealed.

To qualify for protection, the employee usually has to make the disclosure to you, a government minister, an outside regulator or a legal advisor.

Protection will be still given where a wider disclosure is made, as long as the whistleblower can show that the disclosure was made in good faith, that there was genuine belief that the information was true and that it was reasonable to make the disclosure in the circumstances.

The requirement for whistleblowing to be in good faith means that an employee's chief motive must be to remedy the wrong he has reported. If not (for example, if the dominant motive is personal antagonism), the disclosure will not be protected, even where the information is true.

Example

Ms Street made various allegations of impropriety against her manager. She refused to co-operate with the employer's investigation, which exonerated the manager and was critical of her. She was dismissed and claimed that she had been unfairly dismissed because of her disclosures.

The court considered Ms Street's motive for making the disclosures and concluded that they were motivated by personal antagonism. It said that a disclosure would not be made in good faith if an ulterior motive was the predominant purpose of making it, even if the person making the disclosure reasonably believed that the disclosure was true. Street v Derbyshire Unemployed Workers' Centre [2004]

Employees can complain to a tribunal if they feel that their employer penalises them for bringing the complaint. If they are dismissed because they blew the whistle, the dismissal would be automatically unfair. Compensation is unlimited.

Example

Ms Lingard's disclosure concerned the intimidation and bullying of inmates by a particular prison officer. One reported incident involved the officer threatening a sex offender inmate with prisoner violence should he find images of children in the cell. The employer failed to carry out an adequate investigation, did not respond appropriately to her concerns, failed to keep her disclosure confidential and did not take steps to reduce the risks to her from that failure.

Ms Lingard was awarded a record £477,600 in compensation. The award included future loss of earnings, loss of pension rights and compensation for injury to feelings. Lingard v Prison Service [2004]

In normal circumstances the right to complain of unfair dismissal is only available to employees, but not workers. However, the right to complain of unfair dismissal is extended to workers in cases where the main reason for the dismissal is shown to be because the worker has made a protected disclosure.

As with protection under the discrimination legislation, ex-employees should not suffer a detriment (disadvantage) because they have previously made a protected disclosure, even if the date of the detriment and the protected disclosure are some years apart.

Actions for employers:

- Take careful preventative steps to avoid and manage whistleblowing claims;
- Publish, communicate and implement your whistleblowing policy;
- Take whistleblowing claims seriously from the outset. Ensure that you investigate claims thoroughly and promptly;
- Stress that you require employees to raise matters at an early stage, rather than investigating the matter themselves;
- Deal with any serious wrongdoing by employees or managers in a timely way;
- Emphasise to managers and employees that victimising people who raise genuine concerns is a disciplinary offence;
- Take steps to protect the identity of those making a disclosure from other employees;
- Accept that the whistleblowers may be genuine and at risk because of their disclosures. Face up to any unpleasant truths that emerge.

32.   Unlawful Deduction From Wages

You may not make deductions from an employee's or worker's wages without the employee's prior written consent, unless one of the following conditions applies.

The deduction is:

- Required or authorised by legislation (for example, income tax or National Insurance deductions); or
- Authorised by the worker's contract, provided that the worker has been given a written copy of the relevant terms or a written explanation of them before it is made; or
- Consented to by the worker in writing before it is made.

Where an overpayment has been made, recovery may be possible if you can show that the overpayment was due to a mistake in fact, for example, an error in calculation. Where an overpayment is made due to a mistake of law, you will not be able to recover the pay. An example of a mistake in law would be where payment is made in respect of an absence and afterwards you realised that you did not have to make that payment.

33. Right To Be Accompanied At Disciplinary And Grievance Hearings

Workers and employees are entitled to have a companion at formal disciplinary and grievance hearings. This may be a fellow worker or a trade union official of their choice, provided that the request to be accompanied is reasonable. They also have the right to a reasonable postponement of the hearing, within specified limits, if the chosen companion is not available at the time you propose to hold the hearing.

There is no right to be accompanied during an investigation meeting.

Companions have the right to:

- Help the employee prepare for the meeting;
- Make representations and sum up on behalf of the person accompanied;
- Ask questions;
- Ask for an adjournment.

They <u>do not</u> have the right to speak in the place of the employee.

34. Statutory Sick Pay

You must pay Statutory Sick Pay (SSP) to all eligible employees and workers for periods of absence of four days or more for a total of 28 weeks in one period of incapacity for work.

To receive SSP an employee must be:

- Sick for at least four or more days in a row (including weekends and bank holidays). This is known as a Period of Incapacity for Work;
- Earning, before tax and National Insurance an amount equalling or exceeding the Lower Earnings Limit (LEL).

From 1st October 2006 any qualifying employee receives SSP. The Age Discrimination legislation removed the requirement that an employee must be aged 16 or over and under 65.

Earnings are averaged over the eight week period before the employee's sickness began. This period may vary slightly depending on whether he is paid weekly or monthly, or at other intervals. If he has just started his job the calculation may be different.

Where an employee is entitled to full company sick pay, he will receive his normal pay, including any entitlement to SSP.

Should the employee not be entitled to company sick pay, for example, through lack of service, entitlement to SSP depends on:

- The number of days of sickness (there is no entitlement for the first three qualifying days);
- Proper notification to the company of the employee's absence through sickness (which he must do before the end of the first qualifying day); and
- Proper provision of medical certificates, i.e. a self-certificate for the first seven days of illness and a doctor's certificate thereafter.

The qualifying days for SSP are those the employee normally works.

35. Statutory Rights Of Employees

There are a number of statutory rights which become applicable when an employment contract is entered into, although a number of these are dependent on length of employment. Employees have all the rights enjoyed by self-employed people and workers. In addition they have the following rights to:

- An itemised pay statement;
- Written particulars of the main terms and conditions of employment;
- Maternity benefits;
- Paternity benefits;
- Adoption benefits;
- Request flexible working;
- Notice of termination of employment;
- Guaranteed pay when laid off;
- Redundancy pay;
- Parental leave;
- Time off to deal with an emergency involving a dependant;
- Time off for public duties, for trade union activities, duties and training and to look for work if declared redundant with at least two years' service;
- Time off for jury service;
- Protected employment rights when the business is transferred to a new employer;
- Claim protection against unfair dismissal;

- Written reasons for dismissal (upon request);
- Protection against dismissal or unfavourable treatment for taking certain actions on health and safety grounds;
- Protection against dismissal for asserting a statutory right;
- Suspension on medical grounds;
- Protection for fixed term employees.

36. Itemised Pay Statement

All employees are entitled to an individual written pay statement, at or before the time of payment. The statement must show gross pay and take-home pay, with amounts and reasons for all variable deductions. Fixed deductions must also be shown with detailed amounts and reasons. Alternatively, fixed deductions can be shown as a total sum, provided a written statement of these items is given in advance to each employee at least once a year.

37. Written Statement Of Employment Particulars

The general rule is that you must give employees a written statement of the main particulars of employment within two months of the beginning of the employment. The statement should include, amongst other things, details of pay, hours, holidays, notice period and an additional note on disciplinary and grievance procedures.

Maternity Rights

The Government's aim of improving the lives of working parents finds further expression with the Work and Families Act 2006. See Section 8 for a summary. At the time of writing, not all the regulations underpinning the Act have yet been drafted so there may be some additional changes which are not mentioned here.

38. Time Off For Antenatal Care

All pregnant employees are entitled to reasonable time off with pay to keep appointments for antenatal care made on the advice of a registered medical practitioner, midwife or health visitor. Antenatal care can include relaxation and parentcraft classes where recommended by a registered medical practitioner.

After the first appointment you can ask to see the employee's appointment card, a certificate from a registered medical practitioner, midwife or health visitor, confirming the pregnancy and an appointment card or some other document showing that an appointment has been made.

39. Ordinary Maternity Leave

An employee is entitled to a period of 26 weeks' ordinary maternity leave, regardless of her length of service.

During the 26 weeks, a woman is entitled to benefit from all her normal terms and conditions of employment, except for remuneration (monetary wages or salary).

40. Additional Maternity Leave

Employees with 26 weeks' continuous service or more by the beginning of the fifteenth week before the expected week of childbirth are entitled to an additional period of maternity leave (AML). The contract of employment continues with limited terms and conditions. The additional maternity leave period runs from the end of the ordinary maternity leave period for another 26 weeks.

From April 2007 the WFA will enable any pregnant employee to take 52 weeks' maternity leave, irrespective of length of service.

Tip: Before she starts her maternity leave, agree with your employee that you will stay in touch. Agree how often and by what method. Once every eight to ten weeks will probably be fine. One of the commonest complaints of women returning to work after maternity leave is that nobody bothered to see how she was doing or to keep her informed. We want to know how she and Junior are doing. In turn we should keep her updated on what's happening in the business, including any training and any job opportunities that may be of interest to her. Note that the Government has echoed this in the Reasonable Contact arrangements in the WFA.

Returning To Work After Maternity Leave

An employee who returns to work after Ordinary Maternity Leave is entitled to return to the same job on the same terms and conditions of employment as if she had not been absent, unless a redundancy situation has arisen. In this case she is entitled to be offered a suitable alternative vacancy or if there is none, redundancy pay.

An employee who is not allowed to return to her job at the end of Ordinary Maternity Leave is entitled to make a complaint of unfair dismissal to an employment tribunal. If she is not given the same job back, she may bring a claim for sex discrimination or a detriment claim in a tribunal. She might also be able to claim constructive dismissal.

An employee who returns to work after Additional Maternity Leave is entitled to return to the same job on the same terms and conditions of employment as if she had not been absent, unless there is a reason why it is not reasonably practicable for her to return to her old job. In this case she should be offered a similar job on terms and conditions which are not less favourable than her original job.

It is good practice for employers to consult with mothers about any proposed changes to their job at the end of their maternity leave if it is possible to do so.

41. Statutory Maternity Pay

A woman is entitled to Statutory Maternity Pay (SMP) if she has worked for you for a continuous period of at least twenty-six weeks ending with the fifteenth week before the expected week of childbirth, and has average weekly earnings at least equal to the lower earnings limit for National Insurance contributions. SMP can be paid for up to 26 weeks. This will be extended by the WFA from April 2007 to 39 weeks and to 52 weeks in 2009-2010. It is payable by you but is partly (or, for small firms wholly) reimbursed by the state. The first six weeks are paid at 90% of her average weekly wage and the balance paid at the current statutory rate.

If a woman has a pay rise that is effective at any time from the beginning of her reference period until the end of her maternity leave her entitlement to SMP must be recalculated.

Example

Ms Alabaster started her maternity leave in January 1996 and received higher rate statutory maternity pay for the statutory period, plus an additional four-week period given as part of her contract of employment. After that she received a flat rate of SMP.

In December 1995, she received a pay increase, but this was not taken into account in calculating SMP because it took effect after the reference period (15 weeks before the due date) used to calculate SMP.

Ms Alabaster complained successfully that her employer's failure to reflect the salary increase in her SMP calculation amounted to sex discrimination. Her employer appealed to the Court of Appeal, which referred the matter to the European Court of Justice.

The court ruled that where SMP is calculated partially on pay received by a woman before her maternity leave starts, a pay rise awarded after the beginning of the SMP calculation reference period and before the end of the maternity leave must be included in calculating the amount of SMP payable. Alabaster v Woolwich plc [2004]

On 6th April 2005, following the Alabaster case, The Statutory Maternity Pay (General) (Amendment) Regulations 2005 came into force. The Regulations confirm that you must ensure that any pay rise awarded to a pregnant employee (or that would have been awarded had she not been on statutory maternity leave) that takes effect at any time between the start of the period used to calculate her statutory maternity pay (SMP) and the end of her maternity leave is reflected in her SMP.

Actions for employers:

- Re-check a woman's entitlement to SMP if she receives a pay rise that is effective either from the beginning of her reference period or the period starting with the beginning of that reference period and ending with the woman's maternity leave;
- She might have more than one pay rise in this period and each will need checking;

- If a woman was not originally entitled to SMP and claimed Maternity Allowance instead, then if your re-checking of her entitlement now shows that she is entitled to SMP, you should pay her the difference between the Allowance and SMP.

42. Maternity Allowance

Women who do not qualify for SMP may be entitled to Maternity Allowance paid by the Department of Social Security for up to 26 weeks. To qualify, she must have been employed or self-employed for 26 weeks in the test period (the 66 week period before the expected week of childbirth), and have specified minimum average weekly earnings.

43. Notification

An employee must give at least 28 days notice of her intention to start maternity leave.

Notification should be made in the fifteenth week before the expected date of the birth. To qualify for maternity leave she must tell you no later than the end of the fifteenth week (known as the Notification Week) before the baby is due to be born:

- That she is pregnant;
- The expected week of childbirth, by means of a medical certificate if requested ;
- The date when she intends to start maternity leave. The woman can normally choose to start maternity leave at any time from the eleventh week before the expected week of childbirth, up to the date of the birth.

Within 28 days of receipt of this notification, you must reply to her in writing giving her the expected return date. The legislation assumes that a woman will take the full maternity leave to which she is entitled. If she is only entitled to ordinary maternity leave the return date will be 26 weeks from the leaving date. If she is entitled to additional maternity pay it will be 52 weeks from the leaving date.

From April 2007 the assumption will be that she will take 52 weeks, irrespective of service.

The pregnant employee is entitled to work up to the expected week of the birth of the child if she is able to do so. If at four weeks before the week in which the child is expected to be born she is ill with a pregnancy related illness, you can compulsorily start her maternity leave. If this happens you will have to recalculate her return to work date.

Women who wish to return to work before the end of their ordinary or additional maternity leave must give 28 days' notice. Under the WFA notice of early return from maternity leave will be extended to eight weeks from four.

44. Risk Assessment

You are specifically required to take account of health and safety risks to new and expectant mothers when assessing risks in work activity. If the risk cannot be avoided, you must take steps to remove the risk or offer a woman suitable alternative work (with no less favourable terms and conditions) if it is available. If this is not possible you must suspend the employee on full pay for as long as necessary to protect her health and safety or that of her baby.

45. Paternity Rights

Employees whose children were born on or after 6 April 2003 have the right to paid paternity leave.

To qualify employees must:

- Have or expect to have responsibility for the child's upbringing;
- Be the biological father of the child or the mother's husband or partner (a female partner of the mother would qualify);
- Have worked continuously for you for 26 weeks leading into the fifteenth week before the baby is due.

You can ask employees to provide a self-certificate as evidence that they meet these conditions.

Eligible employees may take either one or two consecutive weeks' leave (but not odd days).

Leave can start:

- From the actual date of the child's birth; or
- From a chosen number of days or weeks after the date of the child's birth (whether this is earlier or later than expected); or
- From a chosen date.

Leave can start on any day of the week on or following the child's birth but must be completed within 56 days of the actual date of birth of the child.

You will pay Statutory Paternity Pay (SPP) for either one or two consecutive weeks, as the employee has chosen. The weekly rate of SPP will be the same as the current maternity rate or 90% of average weekly earnings if this is less.

The WFA will considerably extend the rights of fathers although the introduction of this right has been deferred until 2009. When it is introduced it is likely that eligible fathers will be entitled to take up to 26 weeks' additional paternity leave. This may be paid. The length of the additional paternity leave and the entitlement to paternity pay will be linked to whether or not the mother has taken advantage of her full entitlement.

Notification Of Intention To Take Paternity Leave

An employee must give notice of his intention to take paternity leave by the fifteenth week before the baby is expected, unless this is not reasonably practicable. He will need to advise:

- The week the baby is due;
- Whether he wishes to take one or two weeks' leave;
- When he wants his leave to start.

The date on which he wants his leave to start may be amended, provided he tells you at least 28 days in advance (unless this is not reasonably practicable).

Employees are entitled to the benefit of their normal terms and conditions of employment, except for terms relating to wages or salary (unless their contract of employment provides otherwise), throughout their paternity leave.

Paternity rights are also available to employees who have adopted a child.

46. Adoption Rights

Adopters have had rights to adoption leave and pay from April 2003. This allows one member of an adoptive couple to take paid time off work when his new child starts to live with them. The other may take paternity leave and pay. This leave is available whether a child is adopted from within the UK or from overseas. An adopted child can be any age from a small baby, up to the age of 18.

To qualify for adoption leave, an employee must be newly matched with a child for adoption and have worked continuously for you for 26 weeks, ending with the week in which he is notified that he has been matched with a child for adoption. This right is not available in circumstances where a child is not newly matched for adoption, for example when a step-parent is adopting a partner's children.

Adopters are entitled to up to 26 weeks' ordinary adoption leave followed immediately by up to 26 weeks' additional adoption leave.

Employees who are proposing to adopt must inform you of their intention to take adoption leave. This should be within seven days of being notified by their adoption agency that they have been matched with a child for adoption, unless this is not reasonably practicable. They should tell you when the child is expected to be placed with them and when they want their adoption leave to start, providing documentary evidence from their adoption agency as evidence of their entitlement to Statutory Adoption Pay (SAP).

You can also ask for this as evidence of entitlement for adoption leave.

If the child's placement ends during the adoption leave period, the adopter can continue adoption leave for up to eight weeks after the end of the placement.

Once you have been notified of the adopter's intention to take adoption leave you must reply within 28 days, setting out the date on which you expect the employee to return to work if the full entitlement to adoption leave is taken. Adopters who want to return to work before the end of their adoption leave period, must give you 28 days' notice of the date they intend to return.

SAP is paid for up to 26 weeks at the same weekly rate as the current maternity pay rate or 90% of average weekly earnings, whichever is the lower. The WFA will extend the adoption pay and return to work notification in the same way and on the same timescale as maternity arrangements.

47. Flexible Working

Employees have the right to request that they work flexibly. They do not have the right to demand it. The right to request a flexible working pattern for eligible employees with children under six or disabled children under 18 places a duty on you to consider such requests seriously and follow a set procedure. You may only refuse a request where there is a recognised business ground for doing so. If you fail to follow a set procedure or decline a request which is not a recognised business ground, you may face a claim.

The request may be for a change in hours and/or times of work and/or to work from home. Parents may make only one request in a 12 month period and once any change has been made it is permanent. There is no right to go back to the original job terms unless it is mutually agreed between the parties.

As an employer, you are under a statutory duty to consider such requests properly. The "duty to consider" consists of a number of procedural steps, and if you fail to go through these steps, the parent will be able to take out a grievance.

Flexible Working To Meet Childcare Arrangements

To qualify for this right, an employee must have six months' service and have children under six (or disabled children under 18). A disabled child is a child in receipt of a disability living allowance. The final time the right may be requested is two weeks before the child's sixth birthday.

The process of applying for a change in working arrangements is as follows:

1. The employee must make a written request. The application must:

   (i) Be made in writing, either on paper or in electronic form;
   (ii) Be dated;
   (iii) Specify that it is an application for flexible working under the flexible working provisions;
   (iv) Confirm that the relationship the employee has with the child entitles them to make the request.

2. Meet with your employee to consider and discuss the issues within four weeks of the request.

3. You should respond in writing within two weeks of the meeting, providing written reasons for the rejection, if applicable. You are able to refuse a request, but you must provide clear business reasons justifying your rejection of the request. Parents may appeal against a refusal.

If you refuse a request, your refusal should be based on one or more of the following grounds.

   ▪ Additional costs;
   ▪ Customer demands;
   ▪ Inability to organize work/staffing;

- Detrimental impact on quality;
- Detrimental impact on performance;
- Inability to find extra staff.

Tip: It isn't enough just to refuse and cite one of the above reasons. Give some detail supporting your decision.

4. The employee has two weeks within which to appeal against such a refusal.

5. The decision on the appeal must be given in writing within two weeks of the date of the appeal.

At every formal meeting the employee has the right to be accompanied by a work-based colleague.

If you don't identify which of the above grounds apply or where the request is rejected on some other ground, an employee may present a complaint to a tribunal. Tribunals are increasingly willing to find cases of indirect discrimination proven and it's difficult to justify refusals of requests for part time work. In one case the employer's requirement that a female employee work at least 75% of her full time hours was indirect sex discrimination, as it was a provision, criterion or practice that had a disparate impact on women and was not justified.

Example

Ms Starmer was a commercial pilot who had been employed by BA since 2001. In 2004 following her return to work after maternity leave she applied to work 50% of her full time hours. BA refused to allow this arguing that she needed to maintain a minimum number of flying hours but stated that she could reduce her hours to work 75% of her full time hours. She lodged an appeal under the company's procedure against her employer's decision but was still unsuccessful. The business reasons given for the refusal included the burden of additional costs, an inability to reorganise work among existing employees, a detrimental effect on quality and performance and an inability to recruit extra employees.

Ms Starmer complained that BA had indirectly discriminated against her on the grounds of her sex. The company appealed unsuccessfully against the decision.

The EAT considered that the original tribunal had correctly weighed up the justifications put forward by BA for requiring that Ms Starmer work 75% of her full time hours, and was not persuaded that BA had satisfied the onus of justifying this requirement.

An issue of safety was considered separately as this was not taken into account by BA at the time of its decision, but raised as part of BA's defence to the proceedings. Safety was considered to be a relevant consideration to the justification argument, even though it did not feature consciously in the decision making process. However, even when considered with all the other justifications put forward for refusing her request, the tribunal concluded that BA had not provided any cogent evidence as to why it would be unsafe or in anyway unsuitable for Ms Starmer to fly at only 50% of full-time hours. British Airways plc v Starmer [2005]

Flexible Working For Other Carers

The existing law, which applies to the parents and some other carers of young and disabled children, will be amended under the WFA to extend the right to request flexible working arrangements to those with caring responsibilities for adult relatives. The revised flexible working regulations will apply from April 2007.

The Government has decided it's not necessary to spell out the nature of the care involved in the legislation. The draft legislation proposes that a carer is an employee who is or expects to be caring for an adult and who is:

- Married to, or the partner or civil partner of the employee;
- A relative of the employee;
- Neither of these but lives at the same address as the employee.

The following two points are not addressed in the draft regulations:

- Is the right limited to one request a year?
- Will the changes result in a permanent change to the employment contract?

No regulations have yet been published. They are expected towards the end of 2006.

48. Notice Of Termination

Under the legislation, both you and your employee are normally entitled to a minimum period of notice of termination of employment. After one month's employment, an employee must give you at least one week's notice. Unless the contract provides for the employee to give longer notice with increasing service, the minimum notice to be given by the employee will remain a week.

You must give an employee at least one week's notice after one month's employment, two weeks after two years, three weeks after three years and so on, up to 12 weeks after 12 years or more. You may both be entitled to a longer period of notice than the statutory minimum if this is provided for in the contract of employment.

Most employees, subject to certain conditions, are entitled to receive payment during the statutory notice period.

Both employers and employees can waive their rights to notice or to a payment in lieu of notice. Either party can terminate the contract of employment without notice if the conduct of the other justifies it.

49. Guaranteed Pay

Guarantee payments were introduced to compensate employees in the event of short-time working. Guarantee payments must be made to employees with at least one month's service, when they could normally expect to work but there is no work is available. Such payments must be made by you for any whole day or days in which work is not available because:

- There is a diminution in the requirements of your business for work of the kind which the employee is employed to do; or
- The normal working of your business in relation to work of that kind is affected by any other occurrence.

An employee laid off in this way is entitled to receive a maximum daily rate for up to five working days in any period of three months. This is reviewed in line with movements in the retail price index.

If the company already has agreed contractual lay-off pay with its employees, the Secretary of State for Trade and Industry may exempt it from these requirements.

Guarantee payments may be withheld if:

- The workless day is the result of industrial action involving any of your employees, or an associated employer;
- The employee unreasonably refuses to undertake suitable alternative work;

- The employee does not comply with any reasonable requirements to ensure that his services are available.

Tip: Any period of lay-off (or short-time working) must be agreed with employees in advance, otherwise you may be in breach of contract.

50. Right To A Redundancy Payment

Redundancy is a dismissal caused by a business' need to cut jobs, restructure the organisation, move the place of work or close down completely.

To qualify for a redundancy payment an individual must meet certain criteria. He must be an employee and must have been dismissed, have at least two years' continuous service on the date on which his notice expires, or if termination is without notice, the date on which termination takes effect.

Where there is a practice of paying enhanced redundancy payments, this may become a contractual right.

Example

Mr Walker was one of 22 employees made redundant by Albion Automotive in January 1999. He did not have a written contract of employment and there was nothing written down about redundancy terms. From 1990 to 1994 there had been six voluntary or compulsory redundancy exercises. In each of these exercises the employer made enhanced redundancy payments whereby redundancy employees received £1,000 for each completed year of service and £90 for each further completed month.

When Mr Walker was made redundant he did not receive the enhanced redundancy payment. He brought a claim for breach of contract to the tribunal. He argued that enhanced redundancy payments had become an entitlement by reason of an implied term in his contract of employment.

The company argued that there was no express agreement to pay enhanced terms.

The court found that an established custom of enhanced redundancy payments was sufficient to establish an intention by the employer to be contractually bound to such payments.
Albion Automotive v Walker & Others [2002]

Redundancy Calculation

The upper age limit for entitlement to a statutory redundancy payment was removed from 1st October 2006. Years of service below the age of 18 now count towards entitlement.

While the provisions for tapering the award between age 64 and 65 have been removed, 20 years' service will continue to be the maximum to count in calculating the award.

An employee still has to have two years' continuous service to qualify for redundancy pay.

Under the age discrimination legislation the calculation of redundancy payments which is based on age, length of service and weekly pay, continues to be lawful if the statutory table under the Employments Rights Act 1996 is used.

For redundancies made on or after 1st October 2006, the amount will be calculated as follows:

- Up to the age of 21 - 0.5 week's pay for each completed year of service;
- 22 - 40 years of age - 1 week's pay for each completed year of service;
- 41+ years of age - 1.5 weeks' pay for each completed year of service

The statutory level for redundancy pay is set annually.

If you choose to enhance redundancy pay, you must make the same adjustments to all three age bands.

51. Parental Leave

The right to take parental leave is given to birth and adoptive mothers and fathers. Employees who have completed one year's service are entitled to 13 weeks' unpaid parental leave for each child born or placed for adoption on or after 15th December 1994. This means that an employee who has twins is entitled to 26 weeks unpaid parental leave.

Parental leave is a right for parents to take time off work to look after a child or to make arrangements for the child's welfare. Parents can use it to spend more time with children and strike a better balance between their work and family commitments.

You can agree your own procedures with your employees for taking parental leave. This can be done by using workforce or collective agreements or through individual arrangements. These agreements will only apply to an employee if it is part of the employee's contract of employment.

Model Scheme

If no other procedure has been agreed, the Government's model scheme will automatically be used. Under this scheme the following provisions will apply:

- In all cases a maximum of four weeks' parental leave in a year can be taken in respect of any individual child;
- 21 days' notice must be given by the employee;

- In most cases, leave must be taken in blocks or multiples of one week based on the employee's normal working week. There is no right to take one day.

Example

Mr Rodway had requested one day off work in order to care for his son, which his employer refused because his job could not be covered. When he took the day off anyway, Mr Rodway received a formal warning following a disciplinary hearing for unauthorised absence. He complained to the tribunal that he had suffered a detriment.

The court held that the minimum period of leave for which an employee could apply was one week. The Regulations specifically refer to a week's leave so the employer was right to refuse Mr Rodway's request and the disciplinary action had been justified. Rodway v South Central Trains Ltd [2005]

The exception to the above is parents of disabled children, who have 18 weeks' leave. They can use their leave in single days over a longer period, up until the child's 18th birthday. They must still give 21 days' notice and the leave is unpaid. Disabled children are those in receipt of a disability living allowance.

If you consider that an employee's absence would unduly disrupt the business, you can postpone the leave for a maximum of six months after the beginning of the period that the employee originally wanted to start his parental leave. Discuss the matter with the employee and confirm the postponement arrangements in writing no later than seven days after the employee's notice to take leave. The notice should state the reason for the postponement and set out the new dates of parental leave. The length of the leave should be equivalent to the employee's original request.

You are not required to keep records of parental leave taken, although you may want to do so for your own purposes. When an employee changes jobs, you are free to make enquiries of a previous employer or else seek a declaration from the employee about how much parental leave he has taken.

You can ask to see evidence to confirm the employee is the parent or the person who is legally responsible for the child. Evidence might take the form of information contained in the child's birth certificate, papers confirming a child's adoption or the date of placement in adoption cases, or in the case of a disabled child, the award of a disability living allowance for the child. Your request must be reasonable, so check the information and make a note of it. It may not be reasonable for you to check on the employee's entitlement every time he asks for leave.

While on parental leave an employee remains employed and some terms, such as contractual notice and redundancy terms, still apply. At the end of parental leave, an employee is guaranteed the right to return to the same job as before, or if that is not practicable, a similar job which has the same or better status, terms and conditions as the old job. Where the leave taken is for a period of four weeks or less, the employee will be entitled to go back to the same job.

Parental Leave Taken Immediately After Birth Or Adoption Of A Child

Parents can start taking parental leave when the child is born or placed for adoption, or as soon as they have completed one year's service, whichever is later. They will be able to take the leave up until the child's fifth birthday, or in the case of adoption, until five years have elapsed following placement.

Parental leave taken immediately after maternity leave cannot be refused. An employee who takes a period of parental leave of more than four weeks straight after the end of either ordinary or additional maternity leave is treated as though she was returning to work after additional maternity leave.

When an employee applies to take parental leave immediately after the birth or adoption of a child, he needs to give 21 days' notice before the beginning of the expected week of childbirth (expectant mothers will be able to provide this information to their partners). In the case of adoption, the employee needs to give 21 days' notice of the expected week of placement. In rare cases where this is not possible, an adoptive parent should give the notice as soon as is reasonably practicable.

52. Time Off For Dependants

Time off for dependants gives an employee the right to reasonable unpaid time off work to deal with an emergency involving a dependent. The right to time off for specified unforeseen circumstances that affect dependants is available to all those who have a contract of employment with an employer, whether they work full time or part time. There is no service qualification.

Examples of unexpected problems:

- If an employee's dependant falls ill or has had an accident or has been assaulted. The dependant does not have to have been physically injured. This right also applies if he has been involved in a situation that has caused him hurt or distress;
- When an employee's partner is having a baby;
- When the employee has to deal with an unexpected hiccough in normal care arrangements, for example, if the child-minder doesn't turn up when expected;
- When the employee has to deal with an incident that involves his child during school time, for example, if the child has been involved in a fight or is being suspended from school;
- If the employee needs to make longer-term arrangements for a dependant who is ill or injured;
- If the employee has to deal with the death of a dependant, for example, to make funeral arrangements or to attend a funeral.

There is no right to take time off under the emergency leave provisions to grieve.

Example

Ms Forster was employed by Cartwright Black for a period of less than one year. At the start of her employment she took five days' sick leave. Some months later she took 12 days' paid bereavement leave following her father's death. Then, a few months later her mother died and she took five days' bereavement leave. When this period expired her doctor signed her off for a total of four weeks.

Cartwright Black dismissed her because of her period of absence following her mother's death and her general absence record with the firm.

Ms Forster lacked the one year's continuous service required to claim unfair dismissal. Instead, she alleged that she had been unfairly dismissed because she took time off in consequence of a dependant's death.

The EAT dismissed her claim on the basis that Ms Forster's absence from work after her mother's death did not fall within the definition of "an action which is necessary in consequence of the death of a dependant". The EAT held that necessary actions covered by the legislation include (but are not limited to) making arrangements such as funeral organisation, funeral attendance, registering the death and applying for probate.

The EAT did acknowledge that a dependant's death will lead to sadness, bereavement and unhappiness, but there is no legal right to compassionate leave as a result of bereavement. Forster v Cartwright Black [2004]

Tip: In these circumstances consider the impact of not providing time off to an employee in such a time of need and the impact on the relations with the employee if you deny time off requested on this basis.

Dependants are people (note that dependents are human, not pets!) who rely on your employee for assistance such as spouse or partner, parent or child. It also includes someone who lives in the same household as a member of the family. This could be an elderly aunt or grandparent who lives in the household. It would not include tenants or boarders living in the family home, or someone who lives in the household as an employee, such as a live-in housekeeper.

In some cases, for example, of illness or injury, this can also include an elderly neighbour who has no one else to support them.

No limit to the amount of leave has been set. Usually, it will be one or two days, but it will vary according to the particular circumstances. Some guidance was provided by the EAT in Qua v John Ford Morrison [2003].

Ms Qua was employed as a legal secretary by John Ford Morrison from January 2000. On 27th October 2000 she was dismissed because of her high levels of absence. Ms Qua complained that she should not have been dismissed on the grounds of her absences as these were caused by her having to take time off to care for her son who had medical problems. She claimed that she was entitled to that time off under the dependency leave provisions and that her dismissal was automatically unfair.

An employment tribunal dismissed Ms Qua's complaint on the grounds that her absences did not count as dependency leave because she had failed to inform her employer of the reasons for her absence as soon as reasonably practicable and/or for how long she expected to be absent. Ms Qua appealed.

The EAT set out guidance for the application of the dependency leave provisions.

- The right is for an employee to take time off to "provide assistance". This does not allow an employee to take time off to care for a dependant personally, except to the extent that this is necessary to deal with an immediate crisis;
- An employee must comply with the notice provisions in order to claim protection. A decision as to whether there has been compliance must be taken with regard to each instance of leave;
- In determining whether time off was necessary a number of factors will be taken into account. These include the nature of the incident that has occurred, the closeness of the relationship between the employee and

dependant and whether anyone else was available to care for that dependant;

- The amount of time that it is reasonable for the employee to take will depend on the circumstances in each individual case. It will always be a question of fact for the tribunal and it is not possible to lay down a maximum reasonable period;

- You are entitled to take previous dependency leave into account when determining whether an employee's absence is necessary and reasonable;

- Time off is permitted when a dependant "falls ill". This does not permit an employee to have an *unlimited* amount of time off. This is so even if the employee complies with the notice requirements each time and only a reasonable amount of time is taken on each separate occasion. The provision does not apply once it is known that the dependant is suffering a particular medical condition and is likely to suffer recurring illness.

However, you should note that you are not entitled to take into account any disruption suffered by the business as the result of the employee's absence. Such inconveniences are (in the eyes of the court at least) irrelevant. To hold otherwise, they said, would undermine the purpose of the legislation.

The right is intended to cover genuine emergencies. No limit on the number of times an employee can be absent from work under this right has been set.

The right is generally for unforeseen matters. If employees know in advance that they are going to need time off, they should ask for annual leave in the usual way.

Employees need to tell you as soon as practicable, the reason for their absence and how long they expect to be away from work. You are not entitled to demand detailed explanations of the reason why an employee can not attend work.

Example

Mr Truelove had to work on some Saturdays. He became aware that his wife would also have to work on a specific Saturday and that their usual childminder would not be able to look after their young daughter on this day. As a result, he asked for the day off as annual leave a fortnight before it was required. This request was refused because there weren't enough staff to cover the work that day. Mr Truelove made alternative arrangements, but these fell through the day before the child needed to be looked after. He mentioned to his manager on the Friday that it was possible he would need to take the following day off to look after his young child. Once Mr Truelove knew that he would be required to stay at home to look after his daughter, he asked another manager for the time off but didn't mention that it was because child care arrangements had fallen through at the last minute. His request was refused.

He was disciplined for taking unauthorised leave and lost his entitlement to a bonus of approximately £250.

He complained that he had been unreasonably refused time off for dependant care leave.

The EAT said that the Act was aimed at helping people who were faced with sudden and difficult situations in respect of a dependant, in this case a child. In this situation, all that the employee had to do was supply enough information for the employer to understand that something had happened to disrupt what had been a stable arrangement in relation to a dependent, and that as a result of this, the employee would have to leave work urgently. The EAT also held, that in this case Safeway Stores had received sufficient information between the various managers to determine that the statutory right to dependant care leave had been engaged. Truelove v Safeway Stores plc [2005]

There may be exceptional circumstances where an employee returns to work before it was possible to contact you, but he should still tell you the reason for the absence on returning.

If you think that an employee is abusing the right to time off you should deal with the situation according to your normal disciplinary procedures. Investigate and consider matters fully before taking action. It is unfair to be dismissed or selected for redundancy for taking, or seeking to take, time off under this right.

Note that there is no statutory requirement for employees to produce evidence, either of the actual incident or their relationship to a dependant.

53. Time Off Work For Public Duties

In certain circumstances you must allow employees who hold certain public positions reasonable time off to perform the duties associated with them. Most of these are unpaid.

Examples include:

- A magistrate;
- Member of the following: a local authority, police authority, educational governing body, local education authority, health authority or primary care trust;
- A member of any statutory tribunal, an environmental agency, or of the boards of prison visitors.

Example

Mrs Riley-Williams was appointed as a magistrate. She had to serve a minimum of 13 days a year. The company said that was too much time off and some time must be taken as holiday. Mrs Riley-Williams resigned and claimed constructive dismissal.

The court held that the right to time off for public duties has to be assessed on what a reasonable amount of time off would be to meet the requirements of the office. It would be reasonable for Argos to concede the 13 days. Their refusal to do so made her resignation a constructive dismissal. Riley-Williams v Argos [2003]

54. Jury Service

If an employee is called up for jury service you must allow him time off for this. Employees have the right not to be treated unfairly (for example, not being considered for promotion) because of the call-up.

You do not have to pay the employee whilst he is on jury service. He can claim for travel, food expenses and for loss of earnings from the court. You will need to fill out a Certificate of Loss of Earnings to claim for loss of earnings. There are limits on the amount that that can be claimed.

An employee can ask for his jury service to be deferred. It can only be done once and for no more than 12 months from the original date.

Note that as from April 2005 any employee who is dismissed because of being called for jury duty, or being absent from work because of jury duty, will be automatically unfairly dismissed. This will apply to all employees, not just those with a year's service or more. The only exception will be where the employee's absence is likely to cause substantial harm to the business, and the employee has unreasonably refused to request to be excused from the jury service.

55. Time Off When At Risk Of Redundancy

An employee who is given notice of dismissal because of redundancy is entitled to reasonable time off with pay during working hours to look for another job, or to make arrangements for training for future employment. The time off must be allowed before the employee's period of notice expires.

Employees are entitled to time off in this way if on a specified date they have had two years' continuous employment.

The date referred to is either the date when the employee's notice expires or the date when the statutory minimum period of notice due under the legislation expires, whichever is the later.

The employee is allowed "reasonable" time off. The legislation does not specify what is reasonable. The amount of time off will vary with the differing circumstances of employers and employees. The courts have indicated that this might be two or three days per week, but it depends on the circumstances. Some employees may need only to attend one interview or make one visit. Others may have to make a number of visits, which may involve travelling distance.

Payment For Time Off

Employees should be paid the appropriate hourly rate for the period of absence from work. This is arrived at by dividing the amount of a week's pay by the number of the employee's normal working hours in the week.

A week's pay is calculated by reference to a date known as 'the calculation date'. In calculating pay for time off to look for work or arrange training, this date is the date on which you gave him notice.

You don't have to pay more than once for the same period. Any payment already made under an employee's contract of employment for a period of time off to look for work will be offset against your liability as an employer under the provisions.

The entitlement to paid time off is limited to 40% of a week's pay for the whole notice period.

Other Time Off – Military Reservists

During peace time military reservists attend an annual camp for training. You may require it to be taken as annual holiday or grant additional time off, either paid or unpaid.

Under the Reserve Forces Act 1996, reservists can be mobilised into full-time service with the regular forces to assist in military operations. An employee who chooses to volunteer for service will have to obtain your permission. However, in the event of a compulsory mobilisation, your consent will not be required.

Compulsory mobilisation may take place where, for example, it appears that national danger is imminent or war-like operations are in preparation. You will be notified by the Ministry of Defence of the date and possible duration of the mobilisation.

You have the right to seek a deferral or exemption from your employee's call-up, on the basis that his absence would cause serious harm to the business, which could not be prevented by the granting of financial assistance. Serious harm could include loss of sales or reputation, a serious impairment to the production of goods or demonstrable harm to the research and the development of new products.

56. Civil Partnerships

The civil partnerships law, which came into force in December 2005, means benefits offered to married employees must be provided to employees who are civil partners. This includes benefits such as survivor pensions, flexible working, statutory paternity pay, paternity and adoption leave, health insurance or time off before or after marriage/registration.

There are no legal requirements to offer such benefits to couples of either the same or opposite sex who have not entered into a marriage or civil partnership. However, where benefits are made available to unmarried couples of the opposite sex, they must be extended equally to same sex couples who have not registered a civil partnership.

Actions for employers:

- Revise all policies to incorporate civil partners' rights and make clear that where the words "spouses" and "marriage" are used, this includes civil partners and civil partnerships;
- Ensure that employees know how to claim any relevant benefits and that any occupational pension scheme gives the same benefits to civil partners as to widows and widowers;
- Avoid forcing people to identify themselves as either married or in a civil partnership.

57. Transfer Of A Business Or Undertaking

The Transfer of Undertakings (Protection of Employment) Regulations 2006, known as TUPE, entirely replaces the Transfer of Undertakings (Protection of Employment) Regulations 1981. The purpose of the legislation is to protect the rights of employees in a transfer situation, enabling them to enjoy the same terms and conditions, with continuity of employment.

This was a notoriously difficult and confused area of the law. The new TUPE regulations go some way towards clarifying matters.

TUPE applies to "relevant transfers". The two broad categories are business transfers and service provisions changes. Some transfers may fall into both categories.

The business transfer category applies where there is a transfer of an economic entity that retains its identity. An economic entity is an "organised grouping of resources, which has the objective of pursuing an economic activity, whether or not that activity is central or ancillary". There are two considerations:

- Is there a "stable economic entity" that is capable of being transferred?
- Will the economic entity retain its identity after the transfer in question?

To decide if there is a stable economic entity that is capable of being transferred, the factors to consider include:

- Is the type of business being conducted by the transferee (incoming business) the same as the transferor's (outgoing business)?
- Has there been a transfer of tangible assets such as building and moveable property (although this is not essential)?
- What is the value of the intangible assets at the time of the transfer?
- Have the majority of employees been taken over by the new employer?
- Have the customers been transferred?
- What is the degree of similarity of the activities carried on before and after?

If the answer to all (or in some cases several of) the above questions is 'yes', then it is safe to assume that there has been a transfer of a stable economic entity.

A service provision change occurs where:

- Services are contracted out by the owner of the business;
- There is second-generation outsourcing i.e. the owner ends a contract with one contractor and awards it to another; or
- The work is brought back "in-house".

Immediately before the service provision change there must be " an organised grouping of employees situated in Great Britain which has as its principal purpose the carrying out of activities concerned on behalf of the client".

It will not be a service provision change if:

- The contract is wholly or mainly for the supply of goods for the client's use; or
- The activities are carried out in connection with a single specific event or a task of short-term duration.

If a TUPE transfer applies, all terms and conditions of work and continuity of employment should be preserved. This principle applies to all employees who were employed in the entity transferred immediately before the transfer; and those who would have been employed if they had not been unfairly dismissed for a reason connected with the transfer.

A dismissal for a reason connected with the transfer will be automatically unfair unless it is for an "economic, technical or organisational" (ETO) reason. Employees with less than a year's service cannot make a claim for unfair dismissal under TUPE because they have insufficient service.

The ETO defence is one of the few permitted reasons for a refusal to take on the transferor's workforce by the prospective transferee. The reason has to be the main cause of the dismissal, thus making the dismissal justifiable, provided that the employer acted reasonably in all circumstances. If it can be shown that the economic reasons were false and that the workforce was not taken on in order to avoid the application of the TUPE regulations, then the transferee could become liable for potential claims.

Transferors must give the transferee written information about the employees who are to transfer and all their associated rights and obligations. This information includes the identity and age of the employees who will transfer, information contained in the employees' written particulars of employment and details of any claims that the transferor reasonably believes might be brought.

If the transferor does not provide this information, the transferee may apply to an employment tribunal for such amount as it considers just and equitable. Compensation starts at a minimum of £500 for each employee in respect of whom the information was not provided or was defective.

The transferor has a responsibility to conduct a full and meaningful consultation with employees at the earliest practicable time. Failure to conduct consultation results in liability for the payment of compensation which may be up to 13 weeks' pay. The transferor and transferee can both be liable for any award of compensation made by an employment tribunal for failure to inform and consult.

The transferee takes over the liability for all statutory rights, claims and liabilities arising from the contract of employment, for example, liabilities in tort, unfair dismissal and discrimination claims. The exception to this rule applies to criminal liabilities.

The provisions of the Pensions Act 2004 apply to transfers taking place after 6th April 2005. This means that provisions equivalent to the TUPE regulations apply to pension rights from that date. If the previous employer provided a pension scheme, then the new employer has to provide some form of pension arrangement for employees who were eligible for, or members of the old employer's scheme. It will not have to be the same as the arrangement provided by the previous employer but will have to be of a certain minimum standard specified under the Pensions Act.

58. Unfair Dismissal

The general rule is that an employee with 12 months' service has the right not to be unfairly dismissed. There are a number of exceptions to this rule and they are listed on page 290.

If an employee thinks he has been unfairly dismissed he may complain to an employment tribunal.

The complaint will be based on one or both of the following grounds:

- The dismissal was for an unfair reason;
- The dismissal was procedurally unfair.

More detail is given in Chapters 6 and 7.

59. Written Reasons For Dismissal

Employees who have been dismissed and have completed at least one year's continuous employment before the effective date of termination can request a written statement of reasons for the dismissal within fourteen days of the request.

Compensation is payable if you fail to respond.

The exception to this is an employee who is dismissed during her pregnancy or maternity leave. She is entitled to a written statement of the reasons for her dismissal regardless of her length of service and regardless of whether or not she has requested it.

60. Suspension On Medical Grounds

You must take all reasonable steps to ensure your employees' health and safety.

In certain circumstances it means you can suspend employees from work if you think they may be at particular risk. For example, you may suspend an employee if he becomes seriously allergic to a chemical at work, or if you have a newly expectant mother working in a lab that uses radiation.

Your decision should be based on a risk assessment.

If an employee is suspended from work on medical grounds he is entitled to full pay for up to 26 weeks and dismissal during this period is unfair.

No pay is due if the employee:

- Is actually bodily or mentally unfit for work;
- Is provided with suitable alternative work, contractual or not;
- Refuses to comply with reasonable requirements imposed by you to ensure his services are available.

61. Protection for Fixed Term Employees

Fixed-term employees have the right not to be treated less favourably than permanent employees of the same employer doing similar work. This protection is given by the Fixed Term Employees (Prevention of Less Favourable Treatment) Regulations 2002, which came into force in October 2002.

Fixed-term employees also have the right to ask for a written statement of reasons for less favourable treatment and can require you to provide such a statement within 21 days of the date of the request.

An employee on a fixed term contract does not have the right to have a contract automatically renewed. However, if you do not renew a fixed-term contract on termination this amounts to dismissal for the purposes of unfair dismissal or redundancy. Employees on fixed-term contracts can no longer waive their right to claim unfair dismissal and/or redundancy payments at the end of the term.

If you hire employees on a series of fixed-term contracts which meet or exceed four years' continuous service, these could be treated as continuous employment in certain circumstances, unless this can be objectively justified.

Originally it was thought that fixed term employees should not suffer less favourable treatment overall, but the comparisons would not necessarily be made on a clause-by-clause basis. Comparators will be permanent employees who are engaged in the same or broadly similar work. These issues were considered in an employment tribunal decision in 2005 and a somewhat different conclusion was reached.

Example

Educational advisors on fixed term contracts enjoyed contractual terms which were overall no less favourable than those enjoyed by their permanent counterparts. Some of the advisors had been working on fixed term contracts for the employer for many years. The contracts of the fixed term employees did not entitle them to enhanced redundancy terms available to permanent employees. The DTI guidance says it may be possible to exclude fixed term employees from redundancy schemes, but Mr Hart, a fixed term employee, successfully argued that it should be a clause-by-clause comparison and consequently they were entitled to the enhanced redundancy pay terms. Hart and others v Secretary of State for Education and Skills [2005]

This decision is not binding but gives an insight into the approach taken by the courts. The tribunal said that the comparison rules should not be interpreted restrictively as this would defeat the object of the phrase "broadly similar work".

Each case must be assessed on its facts, taking into account the employee's skills, seniority and accrued employment rights.

Actions for employers:

- Ensure the time period and project associated with a new fixed term contract are clearly defined and justifiable, so the redundancy of the employee can more easily be proved if the contract is not renewed;

- Avoid giving the employee the same job title or job description as a permanent employee;

- Audit existing fixed term contracts to ensure they do not contain less favourable provisions compared with permanent employees;

- Correct any less favourable treatment or ensure it can be objectively justified;

- Ensure that you carry out the three step statutory dismissal procedure as a minimum level of consultation before deciding whether to terminate or renew;

- Consider whether long serving fixed term employees should be converted to permanent employment status.

62. Children In The Workplace

The main source of health and safety legislation in relation to the employment of a child or young person is the *Management of Health and Safety at Work Regulations 1999*. Under these Regulations the term "young person" means any person under 18.

Before a young person starts work, you must carry out a risk assessment taking into account various issues such as the inexperience and immaturity of the young person, the nature of the workstation, the risks in the workplace including the equipment which the young person will use, and the extent of health and safety training provided.

Young persons cannot be employed to carry out any work which:

- Is beyond their physical or mental capacity (such as heavy manual labour);
- Involves harmful exposure to toxic or carcinogenic agents or radiation;
- Involves the risk of an accident which a young person is more likely to suffer owing to his insufficient attention to safety or lack of experience; or
- Presents a risk to their health from extreme cold, heat, noise or vibration.

No child may be employed to carry out any work whatsoever (whether paid or unpaid) if he is under the age of 14. This is subject to some specific exemptions, for example, in relation to children working in television, the theatre or modelling.

A child may not:

- Do any work other than light work;
- Work in any industrial setting such as a factory or industrial site;
- Work during school hours on a school day;
- Work before 7am or after 7pm;
- Work for more than two hours on any school day;
- Work for more than 12 hours in any week during term time;
- Work more than two hours on a Sunday;
- Work for more than eight hours (or five hours in the case of children under 15) on any day he is not required to attend school, other than a Sunday;
- Work for more than 35 hours in any week during the school holidays (or 25 hours in the case of children under the age of 15); or
- Work for more than four hours in any day without a rest break of at least one hour; or
- Work without having a two week break for any work during the school holidays in each calendar year.

Lastly, if you are considering employing a young person of compulsory school age make sure that your insurance covers the presence of children in the workplace. You must also inform the local education authority in order to obtain an employment permit for that child. Without one, the child may not be covered under the terms of your insurance policy.

63. Smoking At Work

From March 2006 all enclosed workplaces in Scotland became smoke-free. From summer 2007 all public places and workplaces in England will become smoke-free. The Welsh Assembly is planning to introduce similar legislation for Wales.

There has never been a right to smoke at work but there is a right to work in a safe and healthy environment. That includes being protected from passive smoking and increasingly employers have decided to voluntarily introduce smoking bans. From summer 2007 smoking will become unlawful in most workplaces across Britain and this includes company vehicles. Only private homes, care homes, hospitals, prisons and hotel bedrooms will be exempt.

Businesses and authorities failing to comply will be fined £2,500. Spot fines of £200 will be introduced for failing to display no-smoking signs. If the case goes to court, the penalty could rise to £1,000. Individual smokers caught lighting up in banned areas will face a fixed penalty notice of £50.

Some employees may take this opportunity to give up smoking. If that's the case you should do all you can to support their efforts.

Some employees will still want to smoke during working hours and one solution is to allow employees to go outside the building to smoke. This raises certain issues about the amount of time employees are allowed away from their work to smoke. Colleagues may feel it is unfair if smokers get more breaks.

Alternatively you could introduce a complete smoking ban. Employees will only be able to smoke when off the premises before work, after work or during scheduled breaks. If you do decide to go down this route, make sure that you consult and give time to address issues and overcome objections.

Some companies choose to recruit non-smokers. A new European Union ruling has confirmed that companies can legally refuse to employ smokers. (The issue was first raised when concerns were expressed over a job advert placed by an Irish firm which said that "smokers need not apply".) However, the decision was heavily criticised by pro and anti-smoking groups alike. The purpose of recruitment advertising is to trawl the market. Excluding a section because they smoke may not be illegal, but it's not good practice unless there is a clear occupational reason why smoking is not possible.

Actions for employers:

Drawing up a smoking policy may be helpful. You should give consideration to the following matters:

- A preamble giving the reasons for the policy. For example, "This policy has been developed in consultation with workers and their representatives to help provide a healthy, safe and comfortable environment";
- A statement that the policy complies with the relevant legislation (the *Smoking, Health and Social Care (Scotland) Bill 2004* in Scotland;

the *Health Bill* in England and Wales (from summer 2007);

- A statement that the policy applies to workers at all levels;
- The names of those responsible for implementing and maintaining the policy (usually a named manager is given overall responsibility with day to day responsibility resting with supervisors and line managers);
- Information about arrangements for smokers – for example, smoking outside the premises;
- How the organisation will deal with non-observance of smoking restrictions;
- A statement that the policy applies to all visitors and customers.

64. Information And Consultation

The Information and Consultation of Employees Regulations 2004 (known as the ICE Regulations) require employers who qualify to set up a framework for information and consultation if 10% of their workforce request it. If there is a pre-existing information and consultation structure, change can only be made if 40% of the employees request it.

The first stage of the Regulations came into force in April 2005 and affects employers with 150 or more staff. Employers with 100 staff will be included from April 2007 and the remaining group of employers, those with 50 or more staff, will be included from April 2008.

"Information" means data transmitted by the employer either to the information and consultation representatives, or to the employees in order to enable those representatives or employees to examine and to acquaint themselves with the subject matter of the data.

"Consultation" means the exchange of views and establishment of a dialogue between information and consultation representatives and the employer or between the employer and the employees.

There are three categories of information that employers who are subject to the standard provisions must provide to the representatives.

Information must be provided on:

- Recent and probable development of the organisation's activities, developments and economic situation;
- The situation, structure and probable development of the employment within the undertaking and on what measures are envisaged, in particular, where there is a threat to employment within the undertaking;
- Decisions likely to lead to substantial changes in the organisation of work or in contractual relations.

Subjects that might be addressed under "recent and probable developments of the undertaking or establishment" include profit and loss, sales performance, productivity, structure, divestments, market developments and strategic plans.

"Contractual relations" or decisions likely to lead to substantial changes in work organisation could cover:

- Working time and practices;
- Training and development;
- Equal opportunity;
- Health, safety and environment;
- Pension and welfare issues;
- Merger and acquisition;
- Employment plans;
- Transfer of undertakings;
- Collective redundancies;
- Restructuring;
- Reorganisations;

- Data protection issues;
- Outsourcing;
- Pay.

To avoid dispute or confusion, it's a good idea to ensure your information and consultation agreements specify precisely what issues are to be addressed. Note that this includes a duty to consult on changes to occupational and personal pensions.

You don't need to take any action to set up an information and consultation forum unless there is a formal request, although there's nothing to stop you taking the initiative. The procedure is triggered by a request to initiate negotiations to reach an agreement. The default "standard" provisions will apply if an agreement is not reached.

Confidentiality

You can withhold information and not consult where disclosure 'would seriously harm the functioning of the undertaking or the establishment, or would be prejudicial to it'. This means that employee representatives could challenge the withholding of information by employers. You can, however, impose a duty of confidentiality on employee representatives, and this can extend beyond their individual term of office.

If there is a pre-existing agreement the formal request may be blocked.

Pre-existing agreements must:

- Be in writing;
- Cover <u>all</u> employees;
- Have employee approval;
- Set out how you are to give information to your employees or representatives and seek their views on such information.

It is important that a pre-existing agreement contains a sufficiently detailed description of the way in which you will inform and consult with employees.

Example

Moray Council received a request to negotiate an information and consultation agreement from between 10% and 40% of its employees. They took the view that various collective agreements in place together amounted to a pre-existing agreement and duly decided to hold a ballot. Mr Stewart complained to the CAC that this was not the case.

The CAC considered the four conditions and confirmed three were satisfied. The agreements were in writing, they covered all employees (union members and non-members alike, because of the wording of the agreements), and had been approved by the employees. They were also endorsed by trade union representatives who had the right to represent all employees in the undertaking. However the pre-existing agreement did not set out in enough detail how information would be given and views sought.

The agreement stated that it was "a forum for discussion and/or consultation on a range of matters not subject to national bargaining". The CAC thought that was an insufficiently detailed description of the way the council should inform and consult employees. So the council was not entitled to hold a ballot and had to start negotiations right away. Stewart v Moray Council [2006]

Pre-existing agreements may block a valid request which has less than 40% employee support. The employer may hold a ballot instead of entering negotiations and if fewer than 40% of the workforce votes to support the request, the employer is under no obligation to negotiate. The 40% must also constitute a majority of those who actually vote.

If employees want an information and consultation forum they have to fulfil the following requirements:

- There must be a vote by at least 10% of employees in the undertaking;
- There must be a minimum of 15 and a maximum of 2500 employees;
- The 10% can be an aggregate of several requests;
- Aggregated requests must be made within a six month period;
- The request must be in writing;
- The request must be sent to registered office, head office or principal place of business.

Actions for employers:

- Check that current agreements are worded so that they do not suggest they concern consultation only with union members;

- Be able to show that formal documents have been approved if they are not signed;
- Ensure that any agreement, "pre-existing" or otherwise, sets out how the consultation will take place;
- Ensure that you respond to requests for information and give sufficient detail to enable employees to check the information is correct ("verification") and calculate whether employees have the 10% support necessary to make a valid employee request;
- Establish a process for systematic communication;
- Ask employees what information they would like to have;
- Decide who should be responsible for producing this information;
- Decide how far in advance of the meeting it should be supplied;
- Identify any information which you are not prepared to divulge, for example, information relating to an individual or information which is commercially sensitive or confidential.

Tip: Ensure that you stay up to date with all the legal changes and court decisions.

Write to: **subscribe@russell-personnel.com** to receive regular employment updates.

Chapter 5

Managing Absence

65. Introduction

Many employers are reluctant to manage absence, because it can feel uncomfortable – almost invasive – to discuss health issues with employees. Nevertheless, it's really important to take control of any attendance issues. Absence can be a serious drain on a business, with the direct costs alone running to billions of pounds a year across British industry. Unmanaged absence also places a burden on colleagues leading to poor morale if the issue is not tackled, with a consequent reduction in productivity and profitability.

People take time off work for a number of reasons. These can be categorised as:

- Short-term sickness absence (uncertificated, self-certificated or covered by a doctor's certificate). Most sickness absence fits into this category;
- Long-term sickness absence;
- Unauthorised absence or persistent lateness;
- Other authorised absences, for example, annual leave, maternity, paternity, adoption, or parental leave; time off for public or trade union duties, or for emergency leave for dependents; compassionate leave.

Absence comes about for a variety of reasons and may be of varying durations. Tackling it is not always straightforward. You have to develop a range of proportionate responses. There is no one "right" way of going about it but any actions taken by you must always be fair and reasonable.

You must have a system for recording absence otherwise it will be impossible to measure specific types, for example, long term sickness absence. Without the information to indicate the scale of the problem you won't be able to effectively manage the situation.

It can be helpful to identify the persistent offenders (i.e. those with chronic Monday-itis). Someone who takes five days off in one episode is far less disruptive than five one-day absences taken on five separate occasions.

66. Trigger Point

Start managing absence by setting a trigger point, which if met or exceeded triggers an informal investigation and discussion into an employee's attendance.

You can set your trigger where you like. There is no legal limit. You can set very high standards, but your standard is always subject to the over-riding requirement of reasonableness.

Examples Of Trigger Points

Companies have different ways of setting trigger points. Commonly their rules will say something along the lines of "If there are three absences in any six month period (or five in any 12 month period) an investigation will be triggered."

One method used to highlight the persistent short-term offender is the Bradford Factor, which is calculated using the following formula:

$$(number\ of\ episodes)^2\ x\ total\ days\ off$$

Some examples:

- One absence of five days = Bradford Factor 5 (one episode x one episode x five days)
- Five absences of one day = Bradford Factor 125 (five episodes x five episodes x five days)

If used properly, trigger points make attendance visible and high profile. Merely having the discussion with most short term absentees often reduces the problem.

Tip: You can have a challenging attendance standard, but it must be reasonable and achievable.

67. Patterns Of Absence

Once you have set your trigger point, review attendance records regularly (at <u>least</u> every two or three months) and check for the following:

- Regular patterns of absence, particularly Mondays and Fridays;
- Absence on an annual basis, for example, school holidays, public holidays or major sporting events (there always used to be a staggering amount of sickness on Derby Day until the race was moved to the weekend);
- Absences on a certain shifts.

68. Data Protection

The Information Commissioner published Part IV of the "Employment Practices Data Protection Code" early in 2005. This part of the Code is concerned with the processing of information on workers' health (i.e. compliance with the data protection rules when handling information about workers' health). See www.informationcommissioner.gov.uk.

It includes sections dealing specifically with:

- The operation of occupational health schemes;
- The medical examination and testing of workers;
- Drug and alcohol testing; and
- Genetic testing in the workplace.

The following is a summary of some of the Code's provisions:

- Information about workers' health constitutes sensitive personal data under the Data Protection Act 1998 (DPA). This means that one of the sensitive data conditions set out in the DPA must be satisfied before the data can be processed;
- Sensitive personal data conditions will be satisfied if it is necessary for you to process the data in order to comply with your legal obligations, for example, relating to health and safety at work;
- When obtaining the worker's explicit consent to processing data about his health, note that

the consent should be given freely. There must be no penalty imposed for refusing consent;

- Testing for drugs and alcohol must be proportionate to the aim to be achieved and should only be carried out on workers whose drug/alcohol consumption would put the safety of others at risk. So, for example, random testing of train drivers is likely to be justified on safety grounds but the random testing of office-based workers is unlikely to be justified;

- Information about job applicants' health should only be obtained through medical examination or testing if this is necessary to decide whether the worker is fit, or likely to remain fit, to do the job in question. The information should only be sought if it is likely that the applicant will be offered the job;

- Those individuals within your organisation, who are authorised to collect information about workers' health, should be trained to ensure they are aware of the DPA obligations;

- Put appropriate security measures in place to protect information about workers' health. Line managers should only have access to the information they need to allow them to carry out their management responsibilities.

69. Ensure Reporting Procedures Are Followed

As well as setting a trigger point, set clear sickness reporting standards. Most sickness reporting rules say something along the line of, "If you are sick you must notify [named person] by [time] in person." In reality this doesn't often happen and many employees report their absence via a third party. Most sickness absences are for minor conditions and there's no real reason why the sick employee can't notify you in person. If there are exceptional circumstances making it difficult for the employee to report in person, ask about them.

What are your reporting standards? Decide on the following and communicate them to your staff:

- Who should report the sickness absence to the company?
- To whom should the absence be reported?
- By what time?

Tip: Make sure that your employees know and adhere to the reporting requirements (most employees don't and most employers don't challenge it). Don't accept text or email notifications (that's a cop-out).

70. Use Telephone Conversations Positively

When a sick employee phones in, take down as much information as you can. Always be firm, polite and sensitive.

This includes:

- Making a note of the date and time of the telephone call to ensure that your reporting procedures have been followed;
- Asking what is wrong with the employee. What are the symptoms? When did he first experience them? Has he sought (or is he seeking) medical advice?
- Making arrangements to contact him later in the day (or the following day) for a progress report so that you can plan the work schedule.

You can use this data in the return-to-work meeting.

71. Return-To-Work Meetings

If they are well carried out, return-to-work meetings are one of the most effective ways of reducing persistent short term sickness. Unfortunately many managers find them a nuisance or embarrassing and do them so badly that no benefit is achieved.

The whole point of a return-to-work meeting is that the employee feels that he has been missed, that you are concerned about him and want to make sure that things are OK.

Tip: Look **at** the employee when you're talking to him. Smile! You're welcoming him back. Far too many managers develop an unhealthy interest in the papers on their desk or the toe of their shoe when talking to a returning employee. Remember - look him in the eye or the whole conversation loses impact.

Carry out a return-to-work meeting for all employees returning from sickness absence, however short or long the absence. It avoids accusations that you are picking on an individual.

Use the meeting to complete, or sign off any self-certification forms or to collect a doctor's certificate. The completion of a self-certification form is an ideal trigger point for a return-to-work discussion.

Actions for employers:

- Hold the meeting on the day of return. It loses impact the longer you leave it;

- Hold the meeting in private;
- Confirm the reason for the absence;
- Review the attendance record and discuss the facts. In some cases the employee's attendance is generally good, so take the opportunity to thank him for his contribution and note his good attendance;
- In other cases the attendance is not good. If so, get out the attendance record, review it with the employee and express your concern. If there are patterns of absence, ask him to explain them;
- Set out the specific improvement needed;
- Ask whether medical advice has been sought or taken, if this is appropriate;
- Use the meeting to update the employee with job-related information and what happened whilst he was off sick. Let him know that he was missed;
- Update your documentation.

72. Dealing With Persistent Short Term Absence

The best way to reduce short term sickness absence is to highlight it as an issue. Where an employee's absence has exceeded your trigger point, you need to talk to him about it.

Tell him that you are concerned about his attendance and mention that the absence is causing problems.

Investigate the matter thoroughly. First of all try and find out whether the absences are caused by genuine illnesses. Don't put words in the employee's mouth by saying something like, "Are you having problems at home?", but do bear in mind that absences are sometimes caused by domestic or other personal problems. See Chapter 6 for more information on questions.

If the attendance doesn't improve after an informal conversation, take formal disciplinary action. There must be a clear standard for the business and evidence that the employee is below that standard.

It takes persistence but it does work. A client recently told me that after some months of rigorously applying and following through when their trigger point had been exceeded, employees noticed that they have to account for themselves if their absence hit the trigger point ("Do you know what? They sack you here if you take too much time off sick!"). The short term absence has now dropped significantly.

Tip: Stick with it. It works, but you have to maintain the effort.

73. Medical Advice

If the absences are for a series of apparently unrelated reasons, you are not required to take up medical evidence, although it would be a sensible idea to do so before moving on to disciplinary action.

If you write to the employee's GP, you will first need written permission from the employee. Doctors can be very vague so ask specific questions relating to the employee's ill health. The employee has the right to see the report first if he wishes.

A report may indicate that there is an underlying genuine medical condition, which did not originally appear to be the case. On the other hand, there have been some cases where the doctor's report has confirmed that the absentee has not been to the doctor's surgery for some considerable time, indicating that the absences are not all genuine.......

Alternatively, you can refer the employee to your own occupational health advisor. If there is provision for you to do this in the written terms and conditions you won't need to get any additional permission from the employee. If there is no such provision, you will still need to get the employee's written permission.

74. Use The Disciplinary Process

Informal discussion

When the absence reaches unacceptable levels (for example a Bradford Factor trigger point is reached) speak to the employee informally in the first instance and set a time for an improvement. Be precise and clear in your requirements. Don't just talk vaguely about improvements.

Tell the employee what will happen if that improvement is not achieved. Make a record of the discussion.

An employee may accuse you of picking on him because he is sick. Point out that your concern is with his low attendance levels rather than his sickness.

First stage formal warning

If, after an informal discussion, the employee's attendance has not improved to the required standard within the specified time frame, the situation can be moved forward to a first stage warning. At this point the absence problem is often treated as a form of misconduct, and dealt with according to the company's disciplinary procedure.

You can issue warnings related to poor attendance at work. The expected standard of attendance, i.e. the target, must be very clear. Your employee must be given time in which to demonstrate whether he can achieve the specific attendance standard.

Second stage formal warning

If, at the end of the warning period, the employee's attendance has still not reached the required level, continue following your disciplinary procedure. Ultimately this will lead to a final warning. After that, failure to improve to the required standard will lead to dismissal.

Dismissal

It is fair to dismiss for poor attendance, even where the absentee produced a medical certificate for his absences. The dismissal is for a failure to reach a reasonable level of attendance, not about whether the individual was genuinely ill or not.

Example

Mrs Thomson was employed as a racquet stringer. Her record for the first two years of her employment was satisfactory. Thereafter her attendance record became increasingly poor. For the last eighteen months of her employment she was absent on average for about twenty five percent of her working time. Nearly all of these absences were covered by medical certificates. These referred to conditions such as, "dizzy spells, anxiety and nerves, bronchitis, viral infections and flatulence".

She received a number of formal warnings about her persistent absence. These warnings set her targets for improvement and clearly indicated the consequences of failure to improve.

The company consulted their own medical advisor. He could see no common link between the illnesses and said that Mrs Thomson was not suffering from any long-term illness.

When Mrs Thomson returned to work, she was summoned to a meeting and later that day she was dismissed. She claimed unfair dismissal.

The tribunal found that she had been fairly dismissed because she had been clearly advised of the required attendance levels and the consequences of breach. International Sports Co v Thomson [1980]

Tip: This is an old case and these days I would recommend that you do take medical advice before dismissal where possible. There's no legal requirement to do so, but the courts expect it. You would also need to write to Mrs Thomson and give her reasonable time to prepare for the meeting. This is necessary to meet the requirements of the statutory dispute resolution procedures (see Chapter 6).

75. Long Term Sickness Absence

You can fairly dismiss an employee who has long-term health problems, even if he is suffering from a disability. Under the Disability Discrimination Act you must take all reasonable steps to adjust the work and the workplace in order to accommodate the disability. Once you have exhausted the possibilities you do not have to continue to employ a disabled worker when he can no longer carry out his job.

The law does not provide specific time periods for waiting for a sick employee to return to work. Each case must be assessed on its own facts.

Step 1: Set a time limit

Make it clear to your employee that there is a time limit on holding the job open for his return to work.

Your rules should indicate a general time limit for sickness absence after which you will take action. Make sure you clearly tell your employee what your time limit is. Consider taking action when sick pay is about to expire.

Take medical advice.

Step 2: Investigate the alternatives

What can we do to help the employee return to work? Consider:

- Adjustments to the workplace;
- Different work location;

- Change or reduction of hours;
- Equipment;
- Re-training.

Keep a record of these conversations and your efforts to find solutions. You may be able to take advice from a Disability Advisor, contactable through the local Job Centre.

Step 3: Dismissal

If you have reached your deadline and the person is unable to return to work or cope with alternative employment options in the foreseeable future, issue his dismissal notice. Take care to state the reason for dismissal is on the grounds of capability.

76. Workplace Stress

The word "stress" has been used to describe a variety of states, ranging from mild anxiety to serious psychiatric illness. Stress itself is not an illness, but it can be a cause and/or be a symptom of a number of serious illnesses so it should not be ignored. The Health and Safety Executive (HSE) defines stress as:

"The adverse reaction people have to excessive pressure or other types of demand placed on them. It arises when they worry that they cannot cope."

Under health and safety legislation you have a duty to carry out a health and safety risk assessment. This includes identifying risks to mental health as well as physical health. You should take whatever steps you reasonably can to reduce or remove the risks.

The risks of not dealing with workplace stress include:

- Breach of the health and safety legislation;
- Constructive dismissal claims;
- Disability discrimination claims;
- Personal injury.

Example

Managing and working in pubs, bars and nightclubs is a stressful business. Mr Hone was a Licensed House Manager at a SCR pub in Luton. He refused to opt out of the Working Time Regulations and did not agree to work more than 48 hours per week. Despite this his records showed that over a two month period he worked between 89 and 92 hours a week. He complained to his employer that he was working excessively long hours and that he felt tired. They agreed that an assistant manager should be appointed but Mr Hone suffered a collapse before the employer had done anything about the problem. He sued the company for negligence.

Mr Hone had not suffered previous mental illness and had not informed anyone that his health was being affected by the stress of work. However, because he had complained about his workload before his collapse and because the provisions of the Working Time Regulations had been ignored by the company, the court decided that it was reasonably foreseeable that he would suffer a psychiatric injury. Six Continents Retail Ltd v Hone [2005]

For a personal injury claim to succeed against you, an employee must demonstrate the following:

- He is suffering from a clinically recognised illness. The World Health Organisation definition is used;
- It was caused by work related factors;
- You were aware of it and it was reasonably foreseeable;
- You were negligent in your handling of it.

Injuries must be foreseeable. How much can be foreseen depends upon what you know (or ought reasonably to know) about the individual employee. It is not enough for the employee to show that occupational stress has caused the harm. He must show that the breach of duty committed by you, caused (or contributed in a serious way) to the harm suffered.

Example

Mr Walker was a social services manager who had been forced, owing to local authority funding shortages, to take on a far higher volume of work than he could cope with. He suffered a period of being unable to work owing to a stress-related illness. He was offered additional help, but when he returned to work his employer made little or no effort to improve his situation.

He had a second breakdown and was eventually dismissed by his employer.

Northumberland CC argued that it had no reason to foresee that Mr Walker would suffer psychiatric injury. Whilst the court accepted that this might have been the case in respect of the first period of illness, it was perfectly clear that when Mr Walker came back to work he was at risk, and that another nervous breakdown would probably end his career.

The employer's second line of defence was that Mr Walker was unusually susceptible to stress, and that a normal person would not have been so badly affected. The court held that there is ample precedent that the standard of care expected of an employer is raised if the employer knows that an employee is more likely to suffer injury.

A third defence was that, as a matter of policy, it was unreasonable to expect the local authority to hire someone else to share Mr Walker's workload. The authority had a limited budget, and it would be impossible to hire enough staff to ensure that no-one would be overworked.

All of the employer's arguments were rejected by the court. It was simply unreasonable for a local authority to systematically overwork its staff, and then plead funding shortages when they became ill. Walker v Northumberland CC [1995]

There may be warning signs of increased stress levels from employees, for example, higher than usual sickness absences. If an employee actually tells you that he cannot cope, you may be liable for any subsequent breakdown unless you have taken reasonable steps to reduce the burden on him.

77. Voluntary Code of Practice

Reported cases of stress are still increasing and in 2004 the Health and Safety Executive launched a voluntary code of practice to tackle the increasing problem of occupational stress.

This provides a legal basis on which companies can be assessed based on their efforts to reduce stress to acceptable levels. You will be put at risk of legal action if your efforts are deemed to be inadequate.

The code consists of a number of standards. Staff should:

- Be able to cope with the demands of the job;
- Have control over how they work;
- Not be subject to "unacceptable" behaviour;
- Understand their role and responsibilities;
- Be involved in organisational changes.

There should also be adequate staff support. ACAS, the DTI and the HSE have all produced guidelines to help raise awareness of work related stress, reduce the risk and combat it.

Actions for employers:

- Conduct stress surveys to measure stress and its causes. Carry out a risk assessment to identify the risks to the health and safety of any person arising out of, or in connection with, work or the conduct of your business. This includes risks to both physical and mental health;
- While most people respond well to a certain level of pressure, look for the personal and organisational signs that an individual may be under more pressure at work than he can cope with;
- Develop a stress policy, defining stress and containing organisational commitments in order to minimise any potential work-related stress claims. Such a policy would set out guidance to both employees and managers on how to effectively identify and manage stress in the workplace;
- Provide training on stress awareness, coping skills and managing stress;
- Set out the responsibilities of all the parties;
- If possible, offer a confidential counselling service for employees and bring it to their attention;
- Review your employment practices and job specifications and assess whether it is really necessary for employees to work long hours. Regard should be given to the requirements of the Working Time Regulations;
- When appointing a person to a job that may be stressful, explain the stressful nature of the

work and ask him to consider carefully whether he can cope with such demands;

- If it is likely that employees will work long hours, consider asking them to sign the opt-out from the 48 hour week. Note that an employee must not suffer detriment for refusing to opt out;

- Ensure that employees have a reasonably managed workload and that management systems are in place to give them the kind of support they require to carry out tasks satisfactorily;

- If an employee shows signs of stress investigate it. Similarly, if an employee complains that work related stress has caused him an illness or injury, investigate the causes and symptoms with the employee and take appropriate steps to understand the medical issues. Try to establish what has caused the condition and, if it is a work related issue, what you need to do in order to address the cause (if it is possible to do so). Find out what the employee is doing to address the matter and what you can do to help;

- If an employee has been absent from work with stress, it can be helpful to plan for him to return to work in a limited capacity at first, then build up his hours. People are sociable animals and being at home with nothing but daytime TV for company can slow down recovery.

Chapter 6

Discipline And Grievance

78. The Legal Position

In October 2004 the statutory procedures governing disciplinary, dismissal and grievance issues came into place. They affect all businesses regardless of their size, but only apply to employees, not agency staff or casuals.

The statutory dispute resolution procedures form the minimum standard of dispute resolution required from employers and employees (although better contractual procedures will not be affected).

Within the statutory framework there are procedures dealing with discipline and grievance. Under each heading there is a "standard" and a "modified" procedure. These are considered in more detail in the following paragraphs.

There is now an express duty placed upon you to communicate your dispute resolution procedures to employees. The legislation doesn't specify how it should be communicated – it can be by notice board, company intranet, staff handbook or as an attachment to the terms and conditions of employment.

If you don't follow the statutory Disciplinary and Dismissal Procedure (DDP) a dismissal will automatically be unfair. Unlike the other forms of automatic unfair dismissal, the employee must have a year's service to claim unfair dismissal. However, good practice and commonsense suggests that you follow the DDP whenever necessary.

Ensure that all conversations and documents relating to disciplinary or grievance matters are held and managed confidentially.

Requirements Applying To Discipline And Grievance Statutory Procedures

The following applies to both DDP and grievance procedures:

- There should be no unreasonable delay;
- The timing and location of the meeting should be reasonable. For example, a night shift worker should not be required to attend a disciplinary hearing during the day;
- The meeting should allow both sides to explain their case;
- Re-arrange meetings if it is reasonable to do so;
- A more senior manager should hear the appeal if an appeal is lodged;
- Make reasonable adjustments for disabled employees (or for those who may have difficulty understanding the proceedings because English is not their first language);
- The employee has a right to a companion.

Companions

Both employees and workers have a legal right to be accompanied by a workplace colleague or by a union representative during a formal disciplinary or grievance hearing. The right to be accompanied must be offered to employees, but they can choose to waive this right if they wish.

An employee can choose to be accompanied by a union representative even where you don't recognise the union.

Companions have the right to:

- Help the employee prepare for the meeting;
- Ask questions;
- Make representation on behalf of the employee;
- Sum up the employee's case.

They do not have the right to answer questions on the employee's behalf.

Ensure your procedures restrict this right to the named companions listed above.

Compensation

Compensation will be increased by the court where one of the parties has failed to follow the procedures.

The basic award will be four weeks pay, capped at the current statutory rate for a week's pay.

The compensatory award, (compensation for financial loss) will be increased or decreased as follows:

- An increase of 10-50% where you don't comply;
- A decrease of 10-50% where the employee does not comply or fails to appeal.

79. Statutory Disciplinary And Dismissal Procedure (DDP)

This standard procedure will apply where you intend to take disciplinary action (for example, suspension without pay, demotion or loss of pay) in relation to the employee's capability and/or conduct. It will also apply to nearly all dismissals including capability and conduct dismissals, individual redundancies, non-renewal of fixed-term contracts and retirement dismissals.

The standard DDP is a three-step process and involves the following:

Step 1

You must make a written statement of the grounds for action and set up the meeting. This is normally done in the form of a letter:

- Set out in writing the employee's alleged conduct, or other circumstances which lead you to contemplate dismissing or taking disciplinary action against the employee;
- Send the statement or a copy of it to the employee and invite him to attend a meeting to discuss the matter.

Allow the employee reasonable time to prepare. This is not laid out in the DDP, so you must decide what is reasonable in the circumstances. I normally allow a couple of days, but the meeting can be brought forward or deferred by mutual agreement.

Step 2

You must meet your employee to discuss your concerns.

- The meeting must not take place unless you have informed the employee of the reasons for the meeting;
- The employee must have had a reasonable opportunity to consider his response to that information;
- The meeting must take place before disciplinary action is taken, except in the case where the action consists of paid suspension;
- The employee must take all reasonable steps to attend the meeting;
- After the meeting, you must inform the employee of your decision and notify him of the right to appeal against the decision if he is not satisfied with it.

Step 3

The last stage is the right of appeal.

- If the employee wishes to appeal, he must inform you;
- If the employee informs you of his wish to appeal, you must invite him to attend a further meeting;
- The employee must take all reasonable steps to attend the meeting;
- The appeal meeting need not take place before the dismissal or disciplinary action takes

effect. The appeal should be to a different manager;
- After the appeal meeting, the appeal officer must inform the employee of his final decision.

If an employee fails to attend a DDP hearing, you are under a duty to re-arrange the meeting at least once.

Modified Disciplinary Procedure

It is open to you to use a modified procedure. This procedure only applies where the employment has already terminated. It is limited to gross misconduct cases where there is incontrovertible evidence of the employee's guilt, so that having a meeting will make very little difference to the process and the employee is dismissed immediately after the event constituting gross misconduct. The modified procedure should only be used in exceptional circumstances.

Tip: It is recommended that you do <u>not</u> use the modified procedure as there is a strong possibility that such a dismissal will be unfair. It is always a good idea to investigate first then meet to discuss matters before any final actions are taken.

However, if you like living dangerously this is the modified procedure!

- Having dismissed the employee, you must write to the employee about his dismissal;
- Give the employee the right to an appeal.

Exceptions To The DDP

Neither party has to follow the DDP in the following circumstances:

- Where the employee has submitted a claim in the tribunal before a modified dismissal procedure is initiated;
- The case involves a collective redundancy;
- Where the employee has resigned and claimed constructive dismissal;
- The employee is seeking interim relief;
- The employee's dismissal is due to industrial action;
- There is a sudden and unexpected cessation of business (for example, premises burn down) and it becomes impractical to employ any employees;
- Where continuing to employ the employee contravenes a legal duty/restriction imposed by law;
- The employee is covered by a dismissal procedures agreement;
- There has been a dismissal and re-engagement (for example, changes to contractual terms) unless the employee refuses re-engagement.

80. Grievance

A grievance is a ground of complaint raised with you by an employee against another employee or against you.

The traditional way of dealing with a grievance is for a manager to say to an employee, "Well, if you don't like it you know where the door is", which doesn't really solve anything.

It is an employee's right to air a genuine grievance. Every company employing staff, however small the company, must have a process by which staff can formally raise a grievance to your attention. Raising a grievance does not automatically entitle staff to have their own way, but it does require that their issues are properly examined and considered. Many grievances can be dealt with informally by an immediate line manager. Encouraging members of staff to raise their concerns in this way often leads to a quick solution.

Once agreed, make sure that your employees have easy access to a copy of the procedure and that you explain the process to new members of staff, as part of their induction. Do remember to take account of the needs of employees whose first language is not English, or who have a visual impairment or other disability.

Formal Grievance Procedure

If informal discussions are not successful, the employee should raise a formal grievance in writing. If the grievance is against you, it should be raised with a more senior manager or a named alternative person.

Actions for employers:

- Invite the employee to a meeting to discuss the grievance;
- Once you have explored all the issues, respond to the employee's grievance in writing by the deadline given in your company's procedure. You might, for example, expect managers to respond within five working days of the hearing. If the deadline cannot be met, explain the reasons to the employee and say when a response can be expected;
- If dissatisfied, the employee can raise the matter with a senior manager named in the procedure. Depending on the company, this might be a director, the managing director or chief executive. The same principles of holding a formal meeting and providing a response by an agreed deadline apply;
- It is a good idea to identify a third party to whom an employee can take his grievance if it concerns harassment or bullying and he feels he cannot take it to you.

81. Statutory Grievance Procedure

Under the statutory dispute regulations, a grievance is defined as "a complaint by an employee about action which his employer has taken or is contemplating taking in relation to him". It includes actions taken by other employees in respect of the aggrieved employee.

The Three-Step Grievance Procedure

The standard three step grievance procedure is as follows:

1. The employee writes to you about his grievance. This is known as a step 1 letter. Under the standard procedure, the employee is only required to set out the grievance in writing;
2. You set up a meeting to discuss the grievance;
3. If the employee is unhappy with your decision, he can appeal against it.

The Modified (Two-Step) Procedure

The modified version of the grievance procedure entails:

1. The employee writes to you about his grievance. Under the modified procedure, he is also required to set out the basis for the grievance (the grounds of the grievance, as well as the grievance itself), which requires more detail;
2. You respond to the employee in writing.

The two-step modified grievance procedure will only apply where the employee's employment has terminated. Both of you must agree in writing to a "reduced" procedure. There's no meeting or appeal process under the modified grievance process. Like the modified disciplinary procedure, it's best avoided.

The Step 1 Grievance Letter

The idea behind the legislation was that before an employee can raise a claim at tribunal he would invoke the grievance procedure and there would be an opportunity for the parties to sort things out.

The procedure requires a step 1 letter to be issued before an employee can take a complaint to tribunal in respect of a grievance. The only requirement for a step 1 letter is that it has to be written – it can take any form – and refer to the complaint later raised at tribunal. For example, in *Commotion Ltd v Rutty [2005]*, Ms Rutty applied to have her working hours changed, first informally, then formally under the flexible working procedure. Commotion rejected her requests out of hand and she resigned. The court confirmed that her letter requesting to work flexibly could constitute a step 1 letter.

The step 1 letter doesn't have to be written by the employee. It can come from his agent, for example, a solicitor. In *Stewart v Barnetts Motor Group [2005]* a complaint was made in a letter from Stewart's solicitor. It was a found to be a valid step 1 letter because the solicitor was acting as the employee's agent.

The word "grievance" doesn't have to be used in the step 1 letter nor does it have to give a great deal of detail but the complaint must relate to your actions. In *Thorpe v Poat and Lake [2005]* two employees faxed a letter of resignation to their employer which included a "litany of complaints" relating to aspects of the contract. This was enough to qualify as a step 1 letter.

The case law has given us the following guidance:

- The statutory requirements are minimal;
- It is irrelevant whether an employee intended to raise a grievance or not;
- The employee does not have to invoke the grievance procedure;
- The employee does not have to make it plain that the complaint is a grievance or invoke the grievance procedure provided that the grievance is in writing;
- The employee does not have to set out every detail of the grievance – a general outline is acceptable;
- The terms of any company or contractual grievance procedure are irrelevant to whether the statutory process has been followed or not;
- It is not necessary for you to be given a chance to respond before a claim can proceed;
- A questionnaire generated under the discrimination legislation is <u>not</u> a step 1 letter.

Actions for employers:

- The key lesson is that every written communication from an employee that sets out a complaint could be a step 1 letter, even where the employee shows no desire to invoke the statutory procedure;
- In practice you might want to adopt a policy of asking employees to confirm in writing should they wish to raise a grievance. The procedure should set out next steps if they do, including an invitation to a meeting. If you don't do so you may be in breach of the statutory dispute regulations.

General Exceptions To Both DDP And Statutory Grievance Procedure

There will be situations when going through the discussions listed above will be inappropriate. In the following cases neither the statutory disciplinary or grievance procedures apply:

- One of the parties has grounds for believing that starting or continuing with the procedure would result in significant threat to person or to any property;
- One of the parties has been subject to harassment and has reasonable grounds to believe that starting or continuing with the procedure would result in his being subjected to further harassment;
- Where it is not practical to start the procedure or to comply within a reasonable period (for

example, in the case of illness, long-term absence abroad, cessation of business);

- The case involves national security.

82. Extension To The Limitation Period

The limitation period is the time period within which an employee may lodge a claim with the tribunal. The usual limitation period is three months from the date of termination or from the date of the complaint (in the case, for example, of an unlawful deduction or discrimination claim where the employee may still be in employment with you).

Discipline

Employees will be granted an extension of time where they have reasonable grounds to believe that a statutory DDP is still ongoing when the normal time limit expires. This clearly has implications for appeal processes.

Grievance

If an employee lodges an inadmissible claim in the three months after termination of employment or the date of the matter constituting the complaint then he will be granted a three month extension. A claim will be inadmissible if the employee doesn't issue a step 1 letter and wait for a minimum of 28 days (to give you the chance to address his grievance) after its issue before making a claim.

Alternatively, if he has lodged a step 1 letter in the three months following the termination or the complaint then he will be granted a three month extension.

Example

On 3rd December 2004, Messrs Poat and Lake resigned by way of a faxed letter, alleging breaches of their contracts. On 15th March 2005, they lodged tribunal complaints for breach of contract. The company claimed that the complaints were two weeks out of time.

The court found that the faxed letter raised a grievance for the purpose of the statutory dispute resolution procedures, so although the three-month time limit for presenting complaints had passed, the claims were in time. As the statutory grievance procedures applied and the employees had submitted a step 1 letter (setting out their grievance in writing) before the end of the three-month time limit, then the time for presenting a complaint was extended by three months. Thorpe and Soleil Investments Ltd v Poat and Lake [2005]

83. Preventing Problems - Standards And Rules

Standards

A standard is the minimum level of conduct or performance acceptable to the company.

The objective is to provide clear standards and rules, which enhance a productive working environment and improve relationships.

It is important that standards are put across in precise, clear and measurable terms. For example, "The shift start time is 8am". By contrast, saying, "You must be here on time", is an almost meaningless remark.

You need to tell all your workers about the standards that are important to your company. It is good practice to advise prospective employees of key standards at the recruitment stage. For example, if shift work is required, you should tell the candidate about this at the interview. Standards must be reinforced at induction, on a daily or weekly basis, in the workplace and at appraisal.

Rules

Rules are the "dos" and "don'ts" of the workplace.

Disciplinary rules set the standards for the organisation. Rules may specify standards of:

- Punctuality;
- Attendance;
- Performance;

- Appearance;
- Conduct;
- Safety.

Communicate disciplinary rules to all employees as soon as possible so that everyone knows and understands what is expected from them. It's a good idea to cover the rules as part of the induction procedure. Rules should be:

- Written down so that employees know what is required of them and misunderstandings are avoided;
- Fair and should not be discriminatory either in content and in application;
- Accessible. Staff must have access to rules. Make sure that they are set out in your staff handbook, on your company intranet or on your notice board, so that everyone has the chance to familiarise themselves.

Special attention should be given to explaining the rules where work is carried out by young people, i.e. those between the ages of 16 and 18 years, those with little experience of the work, or by staff whose English language skills may be limited.

Disciplinary and grievance rules should be reviewed and updated periodically. Where a rule has fallen into disuse or has not been applied consistently, inform employees in advance of any agreed changes or the reintroduction of the rule.

84. The ACAS Code Of Practice

Disciplinary rules set down the standards that govern the behaviour of employees in the workplace. The disciplinary procedures provide the structure within which the rules are applied.

If you have clear procedures it makes it easier for you to deal with poor performance and misconduct issues.

The Advisory Conciliation and Arbitration Service (ACAS) has issued a Code of Practice on handling discipline at work. Whilst this is not a legally binding document, it is seen as best practice by employment tribunals.

The code recommends a number of features for fair disciplinary procedures. The procedures should:

- Be laid down in writing;
- Specify to whom the procedure applies;
- Provide for matters to be dealt with promptly;
- Indicate the different disciplinary actions which may be taken;
- Specify which levels of management have the authority to take the various forms of disciplinary action. It is good practice to ensure that first line supervisors do not normally have the power to dismiss without reference to senior management;
- Provide for employees to be informed of complaints against them and to be given an opportunity to state their case before decisions are reached;

- Give individuals the right to be accompanied by a trade union representative or a fellow employee of their choice;
- Ensure that, except for gross misconduct, no employees are dismissed for a first breach of discipline;
- Ensure that before disciplinary action is taken, the case is thoroughly investigated;
- Ensure that employees in the discipline procedure are given a full explanation of any disciplinary penalty awarded to them;
- Provide the right of appeal and specify how individuals are expected to appeal.

If you leave out any of the above, you may expect to experience some difficulty if the case is referred to an employment tribunal.

You should also ensure that:

- The procedure applies to all employees irrespective of length of service, unless clearly stated. For example, a short form of the disciplinary procedure may apply during the employee's first year of service;
- The procedure is not discriminatory in application or content;
- There is a provision to suspend employees (with pay) during the investigation stage;
- Where the facts themselves are in dispute, no disciplinary action is taken until the facts have been established.

85. Let The Punishment Fit The Crime

Disciplinary action should be appropriate and a reasonable response to the misdemeanour. You should not give a final warning or dismiss for a first offence unless it is a matter of gross misconduct.

An expired disciplinary warning cannot be taken into account when considering what action to take for a subsequent disciplinary offence.

Example

Mr Thomson was employed in a factory owned by Diosynth, where raw chemicals were processed by way of chemical reactions to produce chemical compounds. The process was highly regulated and there was a constant risk of accidents in the form of explosions or leakage of chemicals. All employees were required to follow Diosynth's safety, and environmental rules of procedure (SHERPS). Mr Thomson was well aware of the rules, had been trained in, and understood the importance of the process he was required to follow in relation to the role he performed.

In July 2000, Mr Thomson was issued with a written warning and was suspended without pay for three days for failing to follow a SHERPS rule which had resulted in a chemical leakage. He assured his manager this was an isolated incident and he would always follow procedure in future. He was told that any failure to do so would result in disciplinary action. The written warning was to last for 12 months.

Fifteen months later, following an explosion in which an operator died, a thorough investigation was carried out into adherence to SHERPS. It was discovered that 18 operators, including Mr Thomson, had failed to follow the same SHERPS procedure that Mr Thomson had previously failed to follow. All 18 operators were disciplined.

Mr Thomson accepted that he had failed to follow the procedure on three specific occasions and had falsified the records to indicate that in fact he had done so. He was dismissed summarily. Diosynth made it clear that without the previous warning, he would not have been dismissed.

The Court of Session found that Diosynth was not entitled to use the time-expired written warning as the basis for taking more serious disciplinary action than otherwise would have been the case.

A warning which is allowed to remain on an employee's record indefinitely will not normally be consistent with good practice.

Additionally, if an employer expresses that a warning is to be valid for a specified period of time, it is unfair to take that warning into account as a determining factor after the warning has expired. Diosynth Limited v Thomson 2006

Actions for employers:

- Handle expired disciplinary warnings with care. Do not rely on them as a key factor in tipping the balance between dismissal and a lesser disciplinary sanction;
- Give thought to the duration of any disciplinary warning at the time it is issued. Bear in mind that it will normally be necessary to fix an expiry date for the warning.

86. Capability ("Can't")

Capability is more about "can't do it" than "won't do it". Sometimes it is difficult to establish if a problem is conduct or capability in origin and you will have to examine the facts of the case closely to determine the reasons.

Dismissal on grounds of capability will be for one of three reasons. These are:

- Lack of ability or skill. This can be repeated minor incompetence or one serious act of incompetence (poor performance);
- Lack of capability because of ill health. This tends to be long term ill health or a situation where an employee's health is declining because of an underlying condition;
- Lack of capability because the employee lacks or has lost an essential qualification.

Tip: An employee would not normally be dismissed for a first incidence of poor performance unless the incompetence demonstrated was gross incompetence, for example, incompetence which was so serious as to be life-threatening.

87. Conduct ("Won't")

Dismissal for a reason relating to the conduct of an employee will be fair, provided the procedure is properly followed.

Examples of misconduct:

- Timekeeping;
- Poor attendance.

Gross misconduct is very serious breach of conduct by the employee. It may be an act or an omission, but it is tantamount to a fundamental breach of contract by the employee.

Examples of gross misconduct:

- Theft;
- Fighting, abusive or intimidating behaviour;
- Consumption of alcohol while on duty.

Your procedure should list the offences you consider to be gross misconduct in your organisation.

88. Informal Discussion

Discipline is intended to encourage employees to meet our standards. If an employee is in breach of a relatively minor rule, you should counsel him to improve. The key issue here is to counsel as soon as a rule or standard has been breached. If you act promptly now, you will probably save time and effort later on. Have one or two informal discussions. If there is no improvement at that point, move to the formal procedure.

Tip: It is <u>not</u> appropriate to have this type of discussion for a serious breach or matter of gross misconduct.

How To Handle An Informal Discussion

This is an informal discussion, so there is no need to offer a companion. Hold the discussion in private. Go through the following points:

- Explain the work standard required;
- Go through the actual performance, giving specific examples;
- Ask for an explanation;
- The purpose of the discussion is improvement, so offer help, support, encouragement and training, as is reasonable and appropriate;
- Agree an action plan for improvement;
- Advise of the consequences of failure to meet the required standard i.e. an escalation to the first formal stage of the disciplinary process;
- Set a timescale for review and diarise;

- Make notes of the conversation. Give a copy of agreed actions to the employee. There is no need to write a formal letter with copy to Human Resources because this is an informal discussion.

Tip: I don't call these informal discussions "informal warnings" because as soon as you bring the word "warning" into the equation it takes you into the formal process. So call it a counselling session (or any of the following: chat, coaching session, conversation, discussion giving advice or guidance).

89. Investigation

When handling any formal disciplinary matter, the starting point is to carry out an investigation.

This should be carried out promptly so that you can collect all the relevant facts before memory fades. Include anything the employee wishes to say. If there are witnesses, take statements from them at the earliest opportunity. Make sure the statements are written, dated and signed. Everyone should be clear precisely what the complaint is.

When reviewing the situation the following issues should be considered (not all of these will be relevant to every disciplinary investigation):

- What is the employee alleged to have done or failed to do?
- What are the circumstances involved. What happened? When did it happen? Who was involved? Where did the incident occur? What were the local, environmental or other relevant conditions?
- What was the job being done by the employee? Is this his normal job?
- How old is the employee?
- How much service does the employee have?
- How long has the employee been in his present job?
- Has the job changed in any way recently?
- Has the employee been counselled about his performance before? Was this recorded?
- What's the employee's past disciplinary history and are there any current warnings?

- Are there any mitigating circumstances?
- Were there any witnesses?
- Has the employee received relevant training?
- What does the employment contract, terms, offer letter and job description say?
- Has any injury or damage been caused by the misconduct?
- What normally happens? Does custom and practice apply?
- Are the standards reasonable and clear? Have they been communicated to the workforce? Can you prove they were aware of the standard required?
- Has the employee got an up-to-date copy of the disciplinary procedure?

90. Suspension

In cases of alleged gross misconduct, consider suspending the employee from work whilst the facts are fully investigated. Suspension must be with full pay and for as short a time as is reasonably possible.

If you suspend staff, make it clear that this is part of the normal investigation process. Employees who are suspended still have the right to be accompanied at a formal disciplinary hearing.

Suspension should only be used where it is really necessary to do so and there is no other alternative. This may involve cases where there is suspected:

- Physical violence;
- Harassment;
- Fighting;
- Fraud or theft.

If there are other options you should consider them before suspending.

Example

Ms Gogay was a residential care worker. A very disturbed child made remarks which could have been interpreted as allegations of abuse. Ms Gogay was suspended whilst an investigation was carried out. As a result of the investigation it was decided that there was no case for Ms Gogay to answer. However, the allegation contained in the suspension letter that the authority was "investigating allegations of sexual abuse", and the effect of the suspension itself, caused

Ms Gogay to suffer a severe psychiatric reaction. The medical evidence was clear that the suspension was a substantial cause of this reaction. There was no pre-existing psychiatric history.

Ms Gogay brought a case based upon a breach of her contract of employment, and in particular the implied terms of trust and confidence.

Even though there was a specific term in the contract allowing for suspensions during an investigation, the Court of Appeal held that suspending someone in these circumstances, particularly with the allegations made in the suspension letter, were calculated to destroy the trust and confidence between employer and employee. It would, therefore, allow a claim for breach of contract unless her employers could lawfully justify their actions. Gogay v Hertfordshire County Council [2000]

Actions for employers:

Suspension does not constitute a breach in itself but it is necessary to consider the circumstances in which it is imposed. These include:

- What was said to the employee about the circumstances justifying the suspension;
- How long the suspension was and whether the employee had lost income because of it;
- Whether the employee had been replaced;
- Whether the contract terms required you to provide work for the employee.

91. Preparation For A Disciplinary Hearing

Give the employee written details of the complaint against him, including witness statements, the procedure that will be followed, and details of the time and place of the disciplinary interview. Remind him of his right to be accompanied by a work-based colleague or a trade union representative.

Tip: The day before the disciplinary hearing check with the employee whether he is ready to go ahead with the hearing. There's no point you, a note taker, a companion and the employee all getting together if the first thing the employee says is that he's not ready to go ahead.

Ensure you have someone with you to take notes.

Collate your information, consider the likely defence and prepare questions.

Questions

The ability to ask the right questions is incredibly useful. Questions help us do so many things:

- Acquire information;
- Check the information for consistency;
- Check our understanding;
- Check the understanding of the other person;
- Build rapport;
- Engage the other person's mind;
- Manage a conversation;
- Regain control of a conversation.

There is a range of question types available to you to use. Choose the type of question that will give you the information you want and allow you to control the pace of the interview.

1. Questions types to use frequently

Open questions

Open questions are essential. They are the basic tool of interviewing. They are called open questions because they open up the discussion, encourage the employee to talk and lead on to more questions. You get much better data, much faster if you use open questions. Once you have asked an open question let the person talk, keep quiet and listen. You need only interrupt with another question if the person is going off the point or not giving you the information you need.

Useful words and phrases:

How	Why
When	Where
Who	What
Describe	Explain
Demonstrate	Give an example
List	Expand on
Tell me	Help me understand …

Tip: Lots of people put, "Can you …." in front of questions and this can have the effect of closing an otherwise open question.

2 Questions types to use carefully

Closed questions

Closed questions are capable of being answered with "Yes" or "No". However, they are useful if you just want to check a fact, for example, "Is your name John?". A simple yes or no would be appropriate.

Leading questions

These can put words into someone's mouth, so may not be a true representation of the facts. An example of a leading question would be "You picked up the bag and went out on to the street, didn't you?"

You can use this form if you are checking or summarizing information that your interviewee has already given you. So, for example, you might say:

"So what you're saying to me is – you heard the fire alarm go, so you picked up your bag and walked after John on to the street? Have I understood you correctly?"

3 Questions to avoid

Multiple choice questions – where you offer a range of answers for the interviewee from which to choose.

Multiple questions – these occur where you ask more than one question at a time.

92. Handling Disciplinary Interviews

Start by checking that the employee is ready to go ahead. Set the scene by describing the structure that the hearing will follow. Make sure that the employee and his companion are informed about the complaint and have copies of all the relevant documentation, for example, witness statements, before the meeting. If you produce items for the first time at the disciplinary hearing, it would be reasonable for the other party to ask for an adjournment whilst he considers the information.

A disciplinary hearing should be a discussion of the facts, not an argument about them. Try and discover whether there are any special circumstances which should be taken into account.

Examine the conduct or performance that is under discussion and explore the gap between the current level of performance/conduct and the required level. Give specific examples to strengthen your argument.

Allow the employee to reply to the allegations.

Take representations from the companion if he wishes to make them.

Be prepared to adjourn the meeting to carry out further investigation if anything new emerges.

Tip: A good question to ask before you close is, "Is there anything else you would like to mention to me that I haven't asked about?"

Once you have heard all the evidence, summarise all the information you have heard from the employee and make any amendments to your notes. Adjourn and carefully consider and weigh the evidence before you decide on any disciplinary action. Ensure that your decision is in line with your policy and procedure and that it is consistent with previous similar situations.

If you decide to issue some form of disciplinary penalty, confirm your decision in writing and tell the employee about the appeals process. He needs to know how to appeal, to whom to appeal and the timescale within which he should submit the appeal.

Discipline is about improvement, so where it's appropriate to do so develop an action plan for improvement. Give a copy to the employee.

A properly conducted disciplinary interview will be a two-way process.

Do not:

- Get involved in arguments;
- Use physical contact or gestures which the employee might regard as threatening;
- Use bad language as this could be seen as bullying or threatening behaviour.

Make sure you follow your procedure. Failure to do so, even if the employee makes an admission of misconduct, is likely to mean that a dismissal is unfair.

Example

Whitbread had employed Mr Hall as a manager of the George Inn, Southwark since 1985. His period of time in charge had been a very successful one. He had won the Evening Standard Pub of the Year Award and received many letters of congratulations from his employer. He had also been sent written warnings from his manager about poor stock control.

After Christmas 1997 Mr Hall went on holiday and instead of carrying out a detailed stock check he "guesstimated" the stock from his holiday residence in Scotland. On his return to London he was asked to attend an investigative interview with his manager.

At the investigation Mr Hall admitted to guessing the stock figures. This misconduct was interpreted by his manager as falsification of company documents, an offence of gross misconduct liable to summary dismissal. Me Hall was dismissed for this and other admitted misconduct offences.

The dismissal was unfair, even though Mr Hall admitted to the act deemed to be gross misconduct, because in dismissing him during an investigation interview and not carrying out a disciplinary hearing, the company had not followed its own procedure. Whitbread Plc v Hall [2001]

Chapter 7

Termination Of Contract

93. Unfair Dismissal

In considering the fairness of a dismissal a tribunal will ask two questions:

1. Was the dismissal for a fair reason?
2. If it was, was it procedurally fair?

In most cases, an employee has to have a year's service qualification to claim unfair dismissal.

Exceptions

The one-year qualifying period does not always apply. There's no service requirement if an employee is dismissed for one of the following reasons:

- Trade union membership or activities or non-membership of a trade union;
- Taking lawfully organised official industrial action lasting eight weeks or less, or for reasons related to trade union recognition procedures;
- Seeking to assert a statutory employment right, such as payment under the NMW or rights under the Working Time Regulations;
- Taking certain specified types of action on health and safety grounds ;
- Pregnancy or for any reason connected with maternity, paternity or adoption;
- Taking, or seeking to take, parental leave or emergency leave for dependents;
- On grounds related to the right to request flexible working;

- Refusing or proposing to refuse to do shop work or betting work on a Sunday;
- Acting as a representative for consultation about redundancy or business transfer, or as a candidate to be a representative of this kind, or taking part in the election of such a representative;
- Exercising, or seeking to exercise, the right to be accompanied at a disciplinary or grievance hearing, or to accompany a fellow worker;
- Performing, or proposing to perform, any duties relevant to an employee's role as an occupational pension scheme trustee;
- Qualifying for working families' tax credit or disabled person's tax credit or, seeking to enforce a right to them (or because you were prosecuted or fined as a result of such action);
- On grounds connected with a spent conviction under the Rehabilitation of Offenders Act 1974;
- Making a protected disclosure within the meaning of the Public Interest Disclosure Act 1998;
- On grounds related to the Part-time Workers (Prevention of Less Favourable Treatment) Regulations 2000;
- On grounds related to the rights of fixed term employees under the Fixed Term Employees Regulations. For example, if a fixed term employee is dismissed because he has requested a written statement of the reasons for his less favourable treatment or because he refused, or proposed to refuse, to forgo a right conferred by the Regulations;

- On grounds connected with information and consultation rights under the ICE Regulations;
- On grounds related to jury service;
- Enforcement of an employee's retirement date where the employee has not been advised in writing of his right to request to work flexibly;
- Dismissal in connection with a transfer of an undertaking that is not an ETO dismissal.

Note that where you fail to follow the statutory Discipline and Dismissal Procedure (see Chapter 6) the dismissal will automatically be unfair. However, the usual one-year service qualification applies so unless an employee falls within one of the exceptions listed above, he cannot bring an unfair dismissal claim if he has less than a year's service.

Tip: To avoid problems and demonstrate best practice make sure you follow the statutory minimum DDP, even if the employee has less than a year's service.

The upper limit for the compensatory award element of the unfair dismissal compensation is index linked and increases annually. The basic award is the same as the statutory calculation of redundancy pay. Occasionally employees are awarded the statutory maximum, but the average level of compensation is around £10,000 for unfair dismissal. Remember that this amount may well be less than what you pay to defend a case. Your final costs could be three times the level of compensation awarded – and you pay your own costs, even if you win the case.

Note that employees dismissed twice and reinstated in-between can date their claim from the <u>second</u> date.

Example

Mr Kirkpatrick was dismissed, reinstated two months later following an internal appeal and dismissed a month later when the employer changed its mind. Mr Kirkpatrick issued an unfair dismissal claim. The question arose as to whether or not continuity of employment was intact during the period between dismissal and reinstatement. It was critical to Mr Kirkpatrick because if continuity was broken his claim based on the original dismissal was out of time and he didn't have the one year's service needed to bring a claim based on the second dismissal. The tribunal established at a preliminary hearing that Mr Kirkpatrick's case could go ahead. The employer appealed.

The EAT held that an employer and employee can agree reinstatement as a matter of contract. That reinstatement will fill the gap in the continuity of employment created by the dismissal, leaving continuity intact.
London Probation Board v Kirkpatrick [2005]

Responsibility Not To Discriminate After Employment Has Ended

Discrimination after employment has ended will still be unlawful, so take steps to prevent it. Although not specified by law, the duty is likely to reduce with the passage of time. Often the responsibility relates to the giving of references (see Chapter 1 for more on references).

Responsibility is not limited to references though. Recently it has been established that liability for sex discrimination can continue after employment has ended.

Example

A model, Ms Walker, was harassed by an employee of BHS, Ms Hough, who was responsible for engaging models on photographic shoots. Ms Walker claimed that Ms Hough came into her hotel room and tried to kiss her. She later sent text messages and invited her to visit a sex shop.

The employment tribunal found that Ms Walker could only claim for the incident in the hotel room as the other later incidents had taken place when she was not employed by the respondent.

However, the EAT disagreed and said that the entire course of conduct alleged was sufficiently close to the employment relationship for BHS to be liable, even though Ms Walker was not employed by BHS at the relevant time. Walker and another v BHS Ltd and Hough [2005]

94. Constructive Dismissal

Constructive dismissal arises where you do, or fail to do, something that causes a fundamental breach in the employment contract ("repudiatory breach"). The employee then resigns in response to the breach and claims unfair dismissal by virtue of the constructive dismissal option.

An employee can resign over one serious incident or as a consequence of a series of incidents. However, the employee must resign soon after the incident in order to be able to rely upon it. Generally your actions must constitute a very serious breach of contract.

To establish constructive dismissal, the employee must show that four conditions have been met:

1. There has been a fundamental breach of the contract caused by you, or there is an intention on your part no longer to be bound by an essential term of the contract;
2. Your breach caused the employee to leave;
3. The employee did not act too soon by leaving before the breach took place. If an employee anticipates a breach and resigns before it happens, he cannot claim constructive dismissal because he hasn't resigned in response to an actual repudiatory breach;
4. The employee did not waive the right to terminate the contract after the breach took place by delaying too long before resigning.

Example

Mr Quigley was a university lecturer at St Andrews. He made a formal complaint about the behaviour of a colleague. In March 2000, he stated that he had taken legal advice and, if he did not get a satisfactory result, he would have "to explore constructive dismissal".

In 2001, Mr Quigley appealed against an unsuccessful application for promotion. While the appeal was pending, a review was carried out. The review concluded that there had been unprofessional behaviour in the department, but no disciplinary action was recommended. Mr Quigley objected to these findings.

His promotion appeal was dismissed in March 2002, and he resigned by a letter dated 29th May 2002. He presented a claim for unfair constructive dismissal on the basis that St Andrews had breached the implied term of trust and confidence.

The tribunal was not satisfied that Mr Quigley had resigned because of the outcome of his appeal or any other alleged breaches of contract by St Andrews. The tribunal took account of the two-month delay between the failure of his appeal and his resignation letter, but did not accept his explanation for the delay, which was that it had taken time to arrange a meeting with a solicitor.

The EAT dismissed Mr Quigley's appeal holding that his delay could not be justified by the time it had taken him to consult a solicitor to discuss his position.

In any event, he had threatened constructive dismissal in March 2000, and so must have been aware of his rights at that time.   Quigley v University of St Andrews [2006]

There are no specific rules about what constitutes a fundamental breach of contract. It is for the court or employment tribunal to determine whether such a breach has occurred, depending on the facts of the situation and the impact on the individual.

Examples Of Constructive Dismissal

- Not supporting managers in difficult work situations;
- Harassing or humiliating staff, particularly in front of other less senior staff;
- Victimising or targeting particular members of staff;
- Changing the employee's job content or terms without consultation;
- Making a significant change in the employee's job location at short notice;
- Falsely accusing an employee of misconduct such as theft or of being incapable of carrying out their job;
- Excessive demotion, disciplining or over-zealous management of employees;
- Refusal of a pay rise to one employee when everyone else got one.

Both employer and employee are under a duty to behave reasonably. Seriously unreasonable behaviour in an employer can constitute constructive dismissal.

Example

Mr Akhtar worked for the United Bank in Leeds. His employment contract contained a written clause which allowed the employer to move employees to any branch within the UK. The United Bank ordered Mr Akhtar to move from the Leeds branch to a branch in Birmingham giving Mr Akhtar six days notice. He requested more time to sort out his personal circumstances, but the employer refused. Mr Akhtar resigned and claimed constructive dismissal.

Mr Akhtar won his case because an employer is under an implied duty to act reasonably. Requiring someone to move in the space of six days is completely unreasonable.
United Bank v Akhtar [1989]

95. Conduct

Dismissal for a reason relating to the conduct of an employee may be fair, but it is vitally important to follow the correct procedure. If you fail to do this, even a dismissal for an apparently glaring case of misconduct could come unstuck.

Example

Mr Murgatroyd worked for the NHS. He was told by his supervisor to stop using his computer for private purposes. This had no effect and the supervisor eventually reported the matter to senior management.

An investigation revealed that Mr Murgatroyd had created over 250 private files on his computer during working hours. He was dismissed and claimed unfair dismissal.

While it was true that Mr Murgatroyd had carried out substantial private work over a period of two years, both before and after the instruction given to him, the tribunal upheld his claim of unfair dismissal. He had not received any indication, let alone a warning, that his conduct could lead to dismissal. There was also evidence that other employees used their computers for private purposes but had not been instructed to stop. Supervision was very lax in relation to this and other matters such as private phone calls and timekeeping.

You must show that misconduct was the reason for the dismissal, following the three stage test in British Home Stores Ltd v Burchill [1980]:

- You believe the employee was guilty of misconduct;
- You have reasonable grounds for that belief;
- At the stage at which you formed the belief you had carried out as much investigation into the matter as was sufficient and reasonable in the circumstances.

Where more than one suspect is involved, the Burchill requirements of genuine belief on reasonable grounds don't apply. Even so, you are still under a duty to carry out the most rigorous investigation you can before reaching a final conclusion.

Example

In a case of suspected theft where more than one employee was under suspicion, the employer investigated but the culprit was unidentifiable. The Court of Appeal found that where two employees are suspected of misconduct and the employer, despite rigorous investigation, cannot discover which is to blame, it may be fair to dismiss both employees on reasonable suspicion short of actual belief. Monie v Coral Racing Ltd [1981]

It is open to you determine what is misconduct (subject always to the over-riding requirement of reasonableness) and that will depend on your business and the standards that you operate.

Typically, timekeeping and poor attendance are examples of misconduct. Theft, fighting, abusive or intimidating behaviour and consumption of alcohol while on duty are all examples of gross misconduct.

Burden Of Proof

The civil burden of proof is the balance of probabilities. This means that on balance it's more likely than not that the employee is guilty of the misconduct. You don't have to have conclusive direct proof of the employee's misconduct – only a genuine, reasonable belief.

96. Capability

Dismissal on grounds of capability will be for one of three reasons.

1. Lack of capability because of ill health.
2. Lack of ability or skill. It could take the form of minor performance problems repeated over a period of time. Alternatively, it could be a single – albeit extremely serious - incident of incompetence.
3. Lack of capability because the employee lacks or has lost a qualification.

You would not normally dismiss for a first matter of competence-related capability unless it was an extremely serious lack of competence.

Example

Mr Taylor was a commercial pilot. He made a faulty landing while flying 77 passengers in reasonable weather conditions. No one was hurt but the aircraft sustained considerable damage. Mr Taylor was dismissed following an inquiry into the incident. He claimed unfair dismissal saying that this was the first incident on a hitherto unblemished record and dismissal was unreasonable in the circumstances.

His claim of unfair dismissal was rejected by the Court of Appeal. Even though it was the first such incident, they pointed out that there are some occupations in which the degree of professional skill required is so high and the potential consequences of the smallest departure from that high standard are so serious, that one failure to perform in accordance with those demanding standards is enough to justify the dismissal.

This was one such case and the dismissal was accordingly fair. Alidair Ltd v Taylor [1978]

97. Redundancy

A redundancy occurs where a dismissal is wholly or mainly because you have ceased to carry out your business or intend to cease to carry out your business:

- Either for the purposes for which the employee is employed; or
- In the place where the employee was employed.

Alternatively, a redundancy occurs where the requirements of that business for employees to carry out work of a particular kind have ceased or diminished or are expected to do so, or the requirements in that place have ceased or diminished or are expected to do so.

Remember that redundancy is still a dismissal. Follow the statutory DDP and include an appeal in the dismissal process.

Do what you can to remove or reduce the need for redundancy, including looking for alternative work opportunities in the organisation. Redundancy can be unfair if you don't provide enough information on other jobs.

Example

Mr Fisher was a New Business Manager employed by Hoopoe. When it ceased trading, he faced redundancy. There was a sales account manager vacancy within Hoopoe's new organisation but no further details were provided as Mr Fisher had expressed no interest in that role.

A few weeks after his dismissal for redundancy, the role was advertised. The financial package was comparable to Mr Fisher's previous position. He claimed unfair dismissal. A key element of his claim was that Hoopoe's failure to provide him with any financial information about the new role meant he was denied the opportunity to give the role any realistic consideration.

The EAT rejected Hoopoe's argument that its only obligation in law was to enquire about job opportunities within the business, and to make any such vacancies known to an employee. Providing such detail as the financial prospects of a particular role should be the norm unless it was not practicable because, for example, the financial prospects had not yet been determined.

However, Mr Fisher's own conduct and lack of interest in the new role indicated that failure by an employee to express an interest in a position or to request further information (including financial information) is a factor that the tribunal may wish to take into account in reducing an award on the grounds of contributory fault. Fisher v Hoopoe Finance Ltd [2005]

Selection For Redundancy

Where a job disappears, or is moved, causing a redundancy, follow a recognised procedure when selecting and dismissing an employee who is to be made redundant.

Before carrying out redundancies, you must:

- Send a written statement, advising the employee of the risk of redundancy;
- Hold a meeting with the employee to discuss the matter. It is usually at this stage that formal notification of redundancy is given;
- Arrange for a more senior manager to hold an appeal meeting if the employee wants to appeal against your decision to dismiss.

Failing to follow the correct procedure means that any dismissal will be automatically unfair. In this case an employee will be able to make a claim for unfair dismissal.

Use a procedure which is fair, objective and non-discriminatory, using a range of objective criteria, such as attendance, disciplinary record, appraisal rating, skills or qualifications.

Consider the following:

- Try to give as much warning of the redundancies as possible;
- Use objective criteria when deciding who will be made redundant and give the employees affected the chance to comment on their scoring against your criteria;
- Try to ensure that the selection for redundancy is fair and in accordance with the criteria set;

- Try to find alternative employment for the employee.

Some employers will have a recognised redundancy procedure which will be part of the contract with workers, and must have been agreed with the trade union at the workplace or with representatives of the workers. In other cases, there may be a procedure which has been consistently used previously and which has not been objected to by the workforce. This will therefore be the procedure that should be followed through custom and practice, unless it is not a fair and/or objective procedure.

Unfair selection for redundancy is a type of unfair dismissal. Someone who has been unfairly selected for redundancy may therefore be able to claim compensation for unfair dismissal as well as redundancy pay.

Collective Redundancies

You have a statutory obligation to consult with employees for at least 30 days as soon as you propose to dismiss more than 20 employees on grounds of redundancy within a 90 day period (or at least 90 days of consultation if it is proposed to dismiss more than 100 employees).

Two decisions must be taken into account when going through the consultation process.

In *Junk v Kuhnel [2005]* the European Court of Justice found that the consultation period must take place before any employees are given notice of dismissal. Previously, it had been understood that it could be legitimate to give notice of dismissal and carry out consultation during the notice period. This reduces the length (and, consequently, expense) of the total redundancy exercise.

In practice it is likely to mean you must defer giving notice until the statutory minimum consultation period has expired.

In the case of *Hardy v Tourism South East [2005]* the court held that there is an obligation to consult where you propose to dismiss 20 or more employees, even when the company intends offering alternative employment to the majority of the employees, i.e. where fewer than 20 employees will actually be dismissed.

In this case, Tourism South East was shutting down one of its sites and planning to relocate some distance away. They relied on the fact that there was suitable alternative employment for most employees, which reduced the numbers affected below the statutory threshold of 20.

The court found that there was a statutory obligation to consult because the employer had proposed to dismiss 20 or more employees. The definition of "proposing to dismiss" was where the employer was proposing to withdraw the existing contract, or the departures the employer was proposing to make from the employees' existing contracts were so substantial as to amount to a withdrawal of the whole contract.

98. Statute

Dismissal by reason of statutory ban is a potentially fair reason for dismissal. The dismissal comes about because the employee cannot continue to work in the position which he held without a contravention, either on the employee's part or on your part, of a duty or restriction imposed by the law.

For example, if you hire a person to work behind the bar of your pub, he must be 18 years of age. If you hire him and discover that he is only 17, you would have to dismiss to ensure you don't fall foul of the law (although you will first be under a duty to investigate to see if you can accommodate him in some other lawful capacity).

It is for you to show that there is a statutory prohibition which makes it impossible for the employee to carry on the same job. That alone is not conclusive of fairness. A tribunal will consider whether you have acted reasonably in dismissing. If you could for example, change the employee's job so that he could do it legally, dismissal is likely to be unfair.

Even if there is a statutory ban, you must satisfy the usual requirement of reasonableness.

Example

Mr Ascroft's duties were partly those of a magistrates court clerk and partly administrative. In 1976 new regulations were issued and he became aware that from 1980 he would be required by law to hold a valid training certificate. This involved passing some exams.

In 1976 he failed the exams. In 1977 he did not re-sit because of a muddle about dates. In 1978 he refused to re-sit, in 1979 he failed the exams and in 1980 he refused to re-sit again. Since he was no longer qualified to sit as a court clerk he was dismissed. The tribunal found that there were no alternative vacancies and Mr Ascroft could not be kept on solely for administrative duties so his dismissal was fair.
Ascroft v Lancashire Magistrates' Courts Committee [1981]

Driving bans are the main cause of statutory ban dismissal. When an employee has lost his driving licence tribunals will normally expect you to consider the following matters before deciding on dismissal:

- Whether driving is an essential part of the job or whether the employee can satisfactorily carry on his duties without a driving licence;
- Whether retaining the employee will mean disruption and inconvenience;
- Whether there is another job to which the employee could be redeployed;
- Whether the employee has had the opportunity to express his views and whether any other suggestions have been reasonably considered.

99. Some Other Substantial Reason

A dismissal for SOSR is a general catch-all category. The statutory discipline and dismissal procedures apply to an SOSR dismissal.

You must show that the reason for the dismissal is a fair one and that you have acted reasonably in dismissing for that reason. Here are some examples:

(a) Dismissal of a replacement for a woman who has taken maternity leave. The dismissal will normally be fair as long as the replacement employee:

- Was informed at the beginning of employment that it would end when the employee taking maternity leave came back to work;
- Was given due notice when employment came to an end;
- Was not dismissed for any other reason.

(b) Business reorganisation. This may sometimes result in a dismissal, but the reason may not be redundancy because the same numbers of people are required to cover a similar range of jobs. Where the dismissal is made for a reason which the employer considers to be a sound business reason, for example, because duties have to be changed to improve efficiency, then this may be accepted by a tribunal.

Example

Mr Lynch was employed as an area sales manager. He worked a five-day week, excluding weekends, with 25 days holiday per year. By 2003 the company had

311

adopted a six-day working week, which Mr Lynch refused to accept. The company eventually wrote to him terminating his current contract on notice but offering him re-engagement on new terms of six days per week and fewer holidays per year. Before his notice period expired, he resigned and claimed constructive dismissal.

The EAT said the company had provided evidence of improved productivity for Saturday working and also its desire to avoid a two-tier system, thereby showing what advantages it expected from its change of policy. This was sufficient to demonstrate a potentially fair reason for dismissal in the form of "some other substantial reason".

There was no constructive dismissal as the changes were not in place when Mr Lynch resigned and, since the giving of lawful notice in accordance with his contract cannot of itself constitute a breach of implied terms, there was no actual or anticipatory breach of contract. Kerry Foods Ltd v Lynch [2005]

100. Summary Dismissal

Summary dismissal is dismissal without notice or pay in lieu following an act of gross misconduct. Gross misconduct is an act which constitutes a fundamental breach of contract by the employee. As a result you may dismiss him without notice, but you must still follow all the usual disciplinary procedures, even if he admits to the gross misconduct.

What constitutes gross misconduct is determined by the company and you should list acts which constitute gross misconduct in your disciplinary procedure.

Every employer's list of what constitutes gross misconduct will be hedged by the caveat "This list is not intended to be exhaustive". This caveat does give scope to dismiss for any particularly heinous act by an employee which doesn't appear on the list. However, you do need to take steps to keep the list updated. For example, with changes in technology "blogging" (keeping an online diary) may become a disciplinary matter. What if a disgruntled employee airs his jaundiced views about you on the world-wide-web in his own time, on his own computer? Can you treat the matter as gross misconduct? Act cautiously if something does arise which isn't on your gross misconduct list but is extremely serious and consider adding it to the list of misdemeanours in your disciplinary procedure.

The employee is entitled to his pay to the date of the dismissal and any holiday accrued but not taken. If the contract contains a clause that allows the company to withhold holiday pay in the event of a dismissal for gross misconduct, it can only be withheld in respect of contractual holiday which exceeds the statutory minimum (four weeks).

Example

Mr Mackay worked for Witley & District Mens' Club as a steward. He had a term in his contract which said that, if he was dismissed on grounds of dishonesty, then the amount of pay for holiday accrued but not taken would be nil. Mr Mackay was dismissed having admitted taking money from his employers and at the time of the dismissal had accrued 26 days' holiday. The club refused to pay this, and Mr Mackay brought a claim in the employment tribunal. The Working Time Regulations) state that an employee is entitled to be paid in lieu of annual leave accrued but not taken at the time their employment ends. The court decided that the agreement not to pay the minimum statutory annual leave accrued under the WTR on the termination of an employee's contract of employment was void and Mr Mackay was entitled to his statutory holiday pay. Witley & District Mens' Club v Mackay [2001]

Instant Dismissal

Dismissing a member of staff without going through the formal disciplinary process, will be an unfair dismissal. Even where an employee is caught red-handed and admits his misdemeanours, a dismissal which takes place without holding a full disciplinary hearing, is likely to be unfair. Always investigate and carry out a hearing.

101. Retirement

Retirement is a new fair reason for dismissal. At, the time of writing it is being challenged in the courts by Heyday and Age Concern.

The default retirement age is set at 65 for men and women. Mandatory retirement before 65 is unlawful unless the lower age can be objectively justified. You don't need to set a retirement age at 65. You can operate with no retirement age, or set a retirement age of 65 or higher.

Employees have the right to be informed of their expected retirement date and of their right to request to work longer. This must be done in writing at least six months, but not more than 12 months, in advance of a planned retirement. Where it has not been done there is a continuing duty upon you to notify up to two weeks before the retirement date. The retirement date is not deferred because of your failure to communicate with the employee. If you fail to do so it means that the dismissal will automatically be unfair.

As part of that communication process employees must be advised that they have the right to request to work beyond any retirement age. A formal request procedure must be used, similar to that used if an employee wants to request flexible working to look after a child.

As a general rule, if an employee makes a request to continue working you must have a meeting with him to discuss his request, notify him of your decision and give him the right to appeal if he is not happy with the decision.

You are not under any obligation to give the employee the right to work beyond his retirement age or provide any reasons for turning down a request to work beyond the intended retirement date because the presumed reason will be retirement.

However, note that you try to dismiss for retirement in any other circumstances the onus will be on you to satisfy the court that the dismissal was for a genuine retirement reason and not, for example, capability or redundancy.

The statutory dismissal procedures will not apply to retirement dismissals. If you fail to comply with your duty to inform an employee of his right to request working beyond the intended retirement date, a tribunal will have the power to make an award of up to eight weeks' pay. A failure to comply with the procedure will also have implications for the fairness of a dismissal.

Tip: If you do give an employee the right to work on beyond his retirement date, consider the use of a fixed term contract which will build in a review date. Where an extension of work is agreed, the "right to request" and "duty to consider" will remain in place when retirement is next considered. This simply means that the right to request to work flexibly will be offered to the employee again. If the employee takes it up, you will have to go through the formal process to consider whether to allow him to remain

Chapter 8

More Tips –Legislation In The Pipeline

In October 2006 the following legislation came into force:

Statutory Dispute Resolution

The Employment Act 2002 (Amendment) Order 2006 extends the scope of the statutory dispute resolution procedures to include information and consultation representatives and representatives appointed under the Occupational and Personal Pension Schemes (Consultation by Employers and Miscellaneous Amendment) Regulations 2006.

Collective Redundancies

The Trade Union and Labour Relations (Consolidation) Act 1992 Act has been amended to reflect the European Court of Justice's decision in *Junk v Kühnel [2005]*, which clarified employers' duties to inform and consult employees before undertaking collective redundancies under the Collective Redundancies Directive.

Family Friendly Matters

The Work and Families Act 2006 has resulted in a number of regulations giving effect to the law.

Maternity And Parental Leave Etc And The Paternity And Adoption Leave (Amendment) Regulations 2006

The Regulations amend provisions relating to statutory maternity leave and adoption leave. The amendments, which apply to an employee whose expected week of childbirth is on or after 1st April 2007, include removing the additional 26 weeks' service qualifying condition for additional maternity leave, so that an employee who qualifies for ordinary maternity leave will also now qualify automatically for additional maternity leave.

Returning To Work Before The End Of Maternity Or Adoption Leave

Note that the following provisions apply equally to employees returning before the end of maternity or adoption leave.

If the employee wishes to return to work before the end of her full maternity leave period (this will normally be the end date you confirmed to her before she went on leave), she must give you eight weeks' notice of her return to work. This notice requirement applies during both ordinary and additional maternity leave. The notice period is the minimum you are entitled to expect, but you can of course accept less or no notice at your discretion.

If the employee attempts to return to work earlier than the end of her maternity leave without giving eight weeks' notice, you may postpone her return until the full eight weeks' notice has been given. However, you may not postpone her return to a date later than the end of her maternity leave period.

An employee whose return has been postponed under these circumstances is not entitled to receive wages or salary if she returns to work during the period of postponement. However, if you failed to provide appropriate notification of when her leave should end the employee is not obliged to give the eight weeks' notice.

Example

If an employee was due to return to work after 52 weeks' maternity leave on 1st August, but then decided to return to work after 39 weeks of leave (that is, on 9th May) she would need to give her employer eight weeks' notice of the new date (that is, by 14th March).

Making Contact During Maternity Or Adoption Leave

Note that the following provisions apply equally to employees on maternity or adoption leave.

During the leave period you may make reasonable contact with an employee, and vice versa. The frequency and nature of the contact will depend on a number of factors, such as the nature of the work and the employee's role, any agreement that you might have reached before the leave began and whether either party needs to communicate important information to the other. An example of this might be news of changes at the workplace that might affect the employee on her return.

The contact between you can be made in any way that best suits you both. For example, it could be by telephone, by email, by letter, involving the employee making a visit to the workplace, or in other ways.

You must, in any event, keep the employee informed of promotion opportunities and other relevant information relating to her job of which she would normally be made aware if she was working.

It's useful to meet before the maternity leave starts, to discuss arrangements for staying in touch with each other. This might include agreements on the way in which contact will happen, how often, and who will initiate the contact. It might also cover the reasons for making contact and the types of things that could be discussed.

What constitutes "reasonable" contact will vary according to the circumstances. Some women will be happy to stay in close touch with the workplace. Others, however, will prefer to keep such contact to a minimum. Encourage such contact as you can. A year is a long time to be out of touch and both parties will benefit from periodic updates.

Work During The Maternity Or Adoption Leave Period – "Keeping In Touch Days"

Note that the following provisions apply equally to employees on maternity or adoption leave.

Employees may, by agreement with you, do up to ten days' work – known as "Keeping in Touch Days" - under their contract of employment during the leave period. Such days are different to the reasonable contact that you may make with one another. During Keeping in Touch Days employees can actually carry out work, for which they will be paid.

Note that the type of work, the number of days (to the maximum of ten) and the dates on which the employee proposes to work is a matter for agreement between both of you. The day may be used for any activity which would ordinarily be classed as work under the contract, for which she would be paid. It could be particularly useful in enabling a woman to attend a conference, undertake a training activity or attend for a team meeting, for example.

When Keeping in Touch Days May Be Worked

Up to ten days' work under the employee's contract of employment may be undertaken at any stage during the maternity leave period by mutual agreement. However, it is not lawful for an employee to work under the Keeping In Touch scheme during the first two weeks after the baby is born (or during the first four weeks if the employee works in a factory).

Payment For Keeping In Touch Days

Because Keeping in Touch Days allow work to be done under the employee's contract of employment, she is entitled to be paid for that work. The rate of pay is a matter for agreement between you, and may be as set out in the employment contract or as agreed on a case-by-case basis. However, you will need to bear in mind your statutory obligations about paying staff, such as ensuring you pay at least the National Minimum Wage and your responsibilities to ensure women and men receive equal pay for work of equal value.

If the employee is receiving statutory maternity pay, you should continue to pay her SMP for the week in which any Keeping in Touch work is done by the employee. You will be able to reclaim reimbursement for some or all of this money in the normal way as before.

If the employee is receiving SMP you may count the amount of SMP for the week in which the work is done towards the contractual pay agreed by the two parties. However, it will always be possible to agree an amount of contractual remuneration over and above the weekly SMP rate to reflect the work the woman has done. This is something that you both need to agree between yourselves before any work is done. Whatever amount of money is paid by the employer in respect of Keeping in Touch Days, you will continue to be able to recover funding for the SMP paid, as normal.

Further advice on statutory maternity pay during Keeping in Touch days is provided by the DWP. Jobcentre Plus provides advice for employees who are receiving maternity allowance.

Statutory Paternity Pay and Statutory Adoption Pay (General) And The Statutory Paternity Pay And Statutory Adoption Pay (Weekly Rates) (Amendment) Regulations 2006

The Regulations amend the Statutory Paternity Pay and Statutory Adoption Pay (General) Regulations 2002 and the Statutory Paternity Pay and Statutory Adoption Pay (Weekly Rates) Regulations 2002. The amendments, which apply to an employee whose child is expected to be placed for adoption with him on or after 1st April 2007, extend the period of adoption pay from six to nine months.

Statutory Maternity Pay and Maternity Allowance (Amendment) Regulations 2006

The Regulations amend the Social Security (Maternity Allowance) Regulations 1987 and the Statutory Maternity Pay (General) Regulations 1987. The amendments, which apply to employees with an expected week of childbirth on or after 1st April 2007, extend the period of maternity pay from six to nine months.

Adoption and Children Act 2002 (Consequential Amendment to Statutory Adoption Pay) Order 2006

The Order amends the Social Security Contributions and Benefits Act 1992 to provide that a person may not elect to receive statutory adoption pay where a child is placed or is about to be placed with him as a member of a couple and his partner satisfies the entitlement conditions for statutory adoption pay and has elected to receive it.

Flexible Working (Eligibility, Complaints and Remedies) (Amendment) Regulations

The Regulations amend the Flexible Working (Eligibility, Complaints and Remedies) Regulations 2002 to extend the right to request flexible working to carers of adults from 6th April 2007.

The definition of a carer will be an employee who is or expects to be caring for an adult who:

- Is married to, or the partner or civil partner of the employee; or
- Is a near relative of the employee; or
- Falls into neither category but lives at the same address as the employee.

The "near relative" definition includes parents, parent-in-law, adult child, adopted adult child, siblings (including those who are in-laws), uncles, aunts or grandparents and step-relatives.

It is expected that the "right to request" process will mirror the existing process followed by the carers of young children.

Disability Discrimination

The Disability Discrimination Act 2005 will be amended from 4th December 2006 as follows:

- Place a duty on public authorities to promote equality of opportunity for disabled people;
- Bring functions of public authorities not already covered by the DDA 1995 within its scope;
- Provide for land based public transport vehicles to be brought within the scope of Part 3 of the DDA 1995;
- Provide for all rail vehicles to comply with rail vehicle accessibility regulations by 1st January 2020, apply accessibility regulations

to refurbishment of rail vehicles and introduce certification and enforcement provisions;

- Subject to consultation, formalise recognition of disabled persons' parking badges issued by other countries;

- Extend the duty of reasonable adjustment, other than in respect of physical features, to those who let or manage rented premises;

- Ensure landlords cannot unreasonably withhold consent for a disability-related improvement to certain rented dwelling houses;

- Extend duties of reasonable adjustment to private clubs with 25 or more members;

- Extend duties of reasonable adjustment to local authorities and the Greater London Authority in respect of their disabled members.

The Corporate Manslaughter Bill, originally expected to be passed in 2006, is now expected to come into force sometime during 2007.

This Bill will create a new offence of corporate manslaughter, which will allow organisations to be prosecuted for management failures that lead to the deaths of employees and others. The new offence will apply when an individual has been killed because the senior management of an organisation has grossly failed to take reasonable care for the safety of employees or others. It will be an offence committed by organisations rather than individuals and would therefore carry a penalty of an unlimited fine rather than a custodial sentence.

2007

On 6th April 2007 the following legislation comes into force:

Information And Consultation of Employees Regulations 2004

In April 2007 the duty on employers to make available a formal information and consultation procedure to all businesses employing at least 100 employees will come into force.

Occupational And Personal Pension Schemes (Consultation by Employers and Miscellaneous Amendment) Regulations 2006

The Regulations introduce a statutory requirement upon employers to consult with prospective and active members of pension schemes and their representatives before making major or significant changes to future pension arrangements. This legislation extends the existing rules to cover undertakings with 100 or more employees.

Work And Families Act 2006

Parts of the Work and Families Act 2006 come into force. The Act extends paid maternity leave from six to nine months for employees with an expected week of childbirth that is on or after 1st April and provides for the introduction of legislation to allow fathers to take up to six months' additional paternity leave (APL), with paternity pay at the standard rate if the mother returns to work before exhausting her statutory maternity pay or maternity allowance.

The length of the APL and the entitlement to paternity pay will be linked to whether or not the mother has taken advantage of her full entitlement.

The intention is that either mother or father will be able to be off work during the first year after the birth of the child. The proposal is as follows:

- Fathers will be entitled to 26 weeks' APL;
- This can only be taken if the mother returns to work before the end of her AML;
- APL will terminate on the date the mother's AML would have ended. This means that if a mother takes some of her AML, the father will not be able to take the full 26 weeks' APL.
- It must be taken in a single block;
- There will be a length of service eligibility requirement;
- The father will receive additional paternity pay (APL) provided that mother had not exhausted her entitlement to SMP and only for so long as that SMP would have lasted;
- There will be flexibility if the mother dies before the child's first birthday.

There will be keeping in touch days during APL.

Note that this part of the WFA has been deferred until 2009/2010.

The Act will also extend the right to request flexible working to employees who care for sick or elderly relatives.

Working Time

On 1st August 2007 The Working Time (Amendment) Regulations 2003 amend the Working Time Regulations 1998 to provide for the 48-hour working time limit for doctors in training to be phased in over a period ending on 31st July 2009. After initially restricting weekly working time limits for doctors in training to 58 hours from 1st August 2004, the Regulations make a further reduction to 56 from this date.

Smoking Ban

A ban on smoking in enclosed public places, including most workplaces, comes into force from summer 2007. The ban is set out as part of the Health Act.

Data Protection

The Data Protection Act 1998 comes fully into force.

Manual filing systems in existence before 24th October 1998 are now required to comply fully with the Data Protection Directive.

Discrimination - CEHR

The Commission for Equality and Human Rights will come into being in October 2007. The body will merge the Commission for Racial Equality, the Equal Opportunities Commission and the Disability Rights Commission, and take responsibility for the new laws outlawing workplace discrimination on grounds of age, religion or belief and sexual orientation. It will also be responsible for promoting human rights. The Equal Opportunities Commission and Disability Rights Commission will be incorporated then, but the Commission for Racial Equality will remain separate until April 2009.

2008

Information And Consultation

On 6th April 2008 the Information and Consultation of Employees Regulations 2004 will be extended. The Regulations, which implement the Information and Consultation Directive in Northern Ireland, are extended to cover undertakings with 50 or more employees.

2009

Working Time

Weekly working time limits for doctors in training reduced to 48 hours from 1st August 2009. The Working Time (Amendment) Regulations 2003 amend the Working Time Regulations 1998 to provide for the 48-hour working time limit for doctors in training to be phased in over a period ending on 31st July 2009. After initially restricting weekly working time limits for doctors in training to 58 hours from 1 August 2004, then to 56 hours from 1st August 2007, the Regulations make a further reduction to 48.

And thereafter ...... during 2009 or 2010 it is envisaged that maternity leave will be extended to 12 months. The Government intends to extend paid maternity and adoption leave to 12 months. This follows the extension to nine months from April 2007.

Most of the forthcoming legislation listed here can be can be viewed on the PSI website (www.opsi.gov.uk)

Tip: Ensure that you stay up to date with the legal changes and court decisions.

Write to: subscribe@russell-personnel.com for our free newsletter containing monthly updates.

Useful Contacts

General

ACAS	www.acas.org.uk	08457 474747
Criminal Records Agency	www.crb.gov.uk	0870 9090 811
Commission for Racial Equality	www.cre.gov.uk	020 7939 0000
DTI	www.dti.gov.uk	020 7215 5000
Equal Opportunities Commission	www.eoc.org.uk	08456 015 901
Health and Safety Executive	www.hse.gov.uk	0845 345 0055
Home Office	www.homeoffice.gov.uk	0870 000 1585
Immigration and Nationality Directorate	www.ind.homeoffice.gov.uk	0870 606 7766

Disability

AbilityNet	www.abilitynet.co.uk	01926 312847
British Council of Disabled People	www.bcodp.org.uk	01332 295551
Disability Rights Commission	www.drc-uk.org	08457 622 633
Employers Forum On Disability	www.employers-forum.co.uk	020 7403 3020
Queen Elizabeth's Foundation	www.qefd.org	01372 841100
Radar	www.radar.org.uk	020 7250 3222
RNIB	www.rnib.org.uk	020 7388 1266
RNID	www.rnid.org.uk	020 7296 8000
SeeAbility	www.seeability.org	01372 755 0000

Notes